Parents belong at the center of a young child's education. The single best way to improve elementary education is to strengthen parents' role in it, both by reinforcing their relationship with the school and by helping and encouraging them in their own critical job of teaching the young. ...Parents need to be able to hold a school accountable for what it does with and to their children. They need to possess the authority to make a change if that change is in their children's best interest.

William J. Bennett
U. S. Secretary of Education

How to Take Control of
Your Child's Education
In the Public Schools

Getting
the Best Bite
of the

by
Linwood Laughy, Ed.D.

Getting the Best Bite of the Apple

by
Linwood Laughy, Ed.D.

Published by Mountain Meadow Press
P. O. Box 1170
Wrangell, Alaska 99929

Cover Design by Bob Parsons, Anchorage, Alaska

Printed in the United States of America

Library of Congress Catalog Card Number: 93-077570
ISBN 0-945519-14-1

Acknowledgments

Grateful acknowledgment is made for permission to reprint previously published material:

Excerpts from *Phi Delta Kappan*: "First Lessons" by William J. Bennett, October, 1986. Reprinted by permission. © 1986, Phi Delta Kappan, Inc.

Excerpts from *Teacher and Child* by Dr. Haim Ginott. Avon (paperback) © 1973. Reprinted by permission of Dr. Alice Ginott.

Excerpts from *Teach Your Own: A Hopeful Path for Education* by John Holt. © 1981 by John Holt. Reprinted by permission of Delacorte Press/Seymour Lawrence.

Table of Contents

Getting the Best Bite
of the Apple

1

Parenting the Public Schools

You can have a dramatic impact on your children's public school education and pave the way for learning success. You don't need a college degree or even a high school diploma. You don't need elegance or community clout. You do need measures of caring, courage and commitment. You do need the willingness to give a few hours each week of your time. You do need the knowledge and skills provided in this book, which will empower you to interact with the public schools in a manner you never thought possible. This book will enable you to get for your children the best available public school education—the best bite of the apple.

"There will be no renaissance without revolution," boldly declared former President Bush as he launched his America 2000 school reform program in 1990. The reform movement of the 1980's had ground to a halt with the recognition that our one hundred fifty year old horse-and-buggy school system would not be significantly improved by keeping the passengers aboard for a longer time or paying the driver more. Thus the 1990s are witnessing a call for school restructuring—the complete redesign of the education system. Meanwhile, however, your child is growing older and his days in school fewer. You need positive change next month, next week, now.

With a January, 1993, article headline, *Parenting* magazine posed the parent's dilemma: "Education: Fight or Flight." Many parents have taken flight to private schools or are supporting school choice initiatives on a state level. Yet for most parents, abandoning the public schools is not any more possible than magically improving the public school system, and many parents feel a strong emotional commitment to public education in our democratic society.

Most, therefore, sit dismayed 'twixt the two alternatives of fight or flight, and their children continue to sit at their public school desks. But a revolution is possible now in the education of your child, and the person—the only person—who can bring about that revolution is you.

Having carefully observed public schools for twenty years—as a teacher, administrator, and parent—I have learned that most parents respond to public education in one of three ways. Let's see who these parents are. Perhaps you are among them.

The Silent Parent

The silent parent engages in no voluntary contact with teachers or school officials. Silent parents are frequently considered by school staff to have no interest in their children's education, which is rarely the case. Some of these parents feel alienated from the public schools due to difficulties they themselves encountered during their own student years—sometimes in the same buildings in which their children now are schooled. Some silent parents feel inadequate to interact with teachers and school officials, and instead rely on these "experts" to make the best decisions for their children. These parents may even avoid routine parent-teacher conferences. Large numbers of silent parents are among the millions of adults in the United States who are functionally illiterate. Still others are simply too busy trying to make a living for their families.

The Angry Parent

The angry parent is confident that the public schools are not deserving of trust and support. The reasons for this attitude often stem from specific local conditions or problems pertaining solely to her child. The angry parent may have attempted unsuccessfully to resolve these problems or may not believe that a resolution is possible. The resultant frustration inevitably leads to anger. This parent's approach to the school may be highly confrontational, or she may simply decide to rely on time to solve the problem—a new teacher, a new principal, or some other change of conditions and actors. At some point, however, the angry parent may abandon the cause and join the ranks of the silent parent.

The Supportive Parent

The supportive parent attends all school functions to which parents are invited, sends goodies for school parties, chaperones at extracurricular events, and may even volunteer to help in the classroom. She joins the Parent-Teacher Association and may serve on a curriculum committee or help with a school bond election. Supportive parents do sometimes recognize that problems exist in public education, including in their local school. They nevertheless believe that school personnel are trying hard to do a good job of educating children, often under difficult circumstances, and suggest that the school deserves the support of all members of the community.

You probably fit into one of these categories. While it is obvious that the third is preferable, I must inform you that all three have one thing in common: they are *ineffective* in ensuring that your child gets the best education possible within the public education system. Happily, there is a fourth alternative.

The Interactive Parent

A small percentage of parents skillfully interact with school personnel to a degree and in a manner that does have a powerful impact on their children's learning. They act to guarantee their children the best bites of the apple. These parents—

- believe in their children's ability to learn;
- are confident that they can influence the educational decision-making that affects their children;
- establish goals for their children's education;
- set high standards for their children's learning;
- methodically interact with school personnel to ensure that their goals and standards are met;

- identify and solve their children's school problems in a carefully planned, systematic way.

You can be an interactive parent. You can master the skills needed to dramatically impact your child's public school education. This book will be your guide. First, we'll look at a key thread that you will weave into all of your efforts: positive relationships with school staff. Next, you'll learn how to spot islands of excellence in the educational sea—to find and secure the best available teacher for your child. Then we'll take a close look at your child's curriculums, the content of her education, and weigh them against your own educational goals for your child. We'll consider ways to set standards for your child's achievement and to honestly and accurately monitor your child's academic progress. Finally, you'll learn a seven-step problem-solving strategy that will consistently lead to positive results.

Results... that's what you'll seek, and with the interactive parenting skills you'll learn in this book, results are what you'll get.

2

Establishing Positive Relationships

As an interactive parent you must, of course, interact. The success of your efforts, as determined by educational results for your child, depends in part upon how well you establish positive relationships with school personnel. For various reasons, this may not be an easy task in today's public school climate.

Teachers, for instance, having lost some of the respect they once enjoyed and having been consistently attacked in the public media, may be sensitive to even a hint of criticism or to the questions and intrusions of parents. Further, teachers are regularly given responsibilities for teaching an expanded curriculum to an ever wider range of students, often with fewer classroom resources. Under such circumstances a critical remark can turn a teacher's sensitivity into frustration and even fury. Educators quickly build defenses against those they feel do not support them, and in the skirmishes that can follow a child may be the first casualty.

On the other hand, one positive segment of school reform in recent years has been what educators may call the parent-involvement movement. Increasingly aware of parents' important role as "first teachers" and necessary partners in the education process, many schools seek to have parents on the school scene, in touch with teachers and involved with their children's schooling. However, despite the proven effects of parent involvement, relatively few parents become truly interactive. Nevertheless, the parent-involvement movement may aid your attempts to be interactive.

You also need to understand that a school is a micro-community, much like a stage play with props and a company of actors. Adults in the school setting typically include the principal, teachers, librarian, school nurse, teacher aides, the school secretary, a counselor, cooks, custodians, maintenance personnel, bus drivers, and sometimes parent volunteers who've become regulars. Also present on an intermittent basis are individuals representing various professional specialties such as a school psychologist or speech therapist. Your child will not have regular contact with all of these individuals, but may frequently deal with staff members other than her classroom teacher. Each of these adults can influence your child's education, and each can be a source of useful information about your child and his program. Before addressing specific means of developing positive relationships with school personnel, let's look at five influential actors in your child's educational world.

The School Secretary

The school secretary plays a central role in the school setting. She frequently controls access to the principal, filters information both to and from the principal's office, and reports her own observations of school events to the principal. She sometimes even offers the principal ideas and recommendations. She may also establish and manage routine procedures of operation, assign students to classrooms, and control parent access to school records. Should she be absent for a day, the importance of her position in the daily operation of the school quickly becomes apparent.

The School Nurse

School personnel maintain health records on your child, primarily to identify any physical problems that could create emergency situations at school (such as epilepsy) and to uncover any physical problems that may affect learning (such as deafness). Some schools may even have a part-time or full-time school nurse. The nurse is in a unique position to observe many aspects of the school's operation and can provide you with valuable insights. He knows which teachers' students try to escape their classrooms with frequent "headaches" or "tummy-aches," which teachers shout at children, the locations on the school grounds and times of day when accidents are most likely to occur, and the possible presence of drugs in the school. The school nurse also monitors your child's general health and is a ready source of information relative to your child's vision, hearing, immunization needs, and general adjustment to school. Further, he will respond to any medical emergency your child may have while at school.

The School Librarian

Children regularly spend time in the school library, not only with their classes but also on an individual basis. The latter is especially true of academically able students, who frequently complete their classwork in much less than the allotted time. The librarian can assist your child in selecting appropriate reading material and can help your child become involved in special learning projects. Library activities may further be available before classes begin in the morning or after school—time which may not otherwise be used productively. Many children, regrettably, never become familiar with the school library beyond checking out an occasional book for a book report. Your relationship with the school librarian can help make the library and its staff a meaningful part of your child's school experience.

The School Principal

The school principal sets standards for both staff and students. She establishes the school's atmosphere relative to student discipline, academic achievement, and teacher competence. She deals with students, staff, parents, and the community at large—frequently filling the air with more juggling pins than you might think could be successfully kept aloft. Recent research on school effectiveness indicates that the principal accounts for a significant amount of the variance in academic achievement among schools otherwise similar in such factors as student composition and the experience level of teachers. Indeed, some studies suggest that the educational leadership of the principal is the *key* factor in the academic achievement of a school. Knowing your school principal's educational philosophies and the depth of her knowledge of current educational methods can provide you with clues to the direction and scope of your child's education. Further, as an ally, your principal can streamline your efforts; but if not an ally, can be a stubborn stumbling block to your interactive success.

The Classroom Teacher

The influence of the classroom teacher on your child's academic achievement, emotional response to learning, and development of values cannot be overemphasized. It was recently reported in the public media that an American child spends an average of five minutes per day alone with his father, forty minutes alone with his mother, and three hours per day engaged with his regular teacher. You also need to remember that your child may have a separate teacher for music, art, physical education, or even reading. You need to identify all these individuals, for each one directly impacts your child's academic and social education. As you interact with school personnel during a given year, remember, too, that somewhere nearby next year's teachers are observing you and your interactive style.

Keys To Successful Interaction

Some important points can now be made to ensure that your contacts with these five school staff members and others will be positive and successful. During your contacts with these people you'll be projecting to them an overall characterization or picture of who you are as an interactive parent, how considerate and determined you are, how carefully you explore the issues, the extent of your genuine interest in your child's education, your willingness to be an active participant, and so on. In other words, over time you'll be sending a general message within which your more specific questions, comments, issues, and actions will be delivered to school personnel. That message should consistently convey, for example, the following points:

- You are seriously interested in your child's education.

- You are a reasonable person, but also firm in your beliefs about what constitutes a quality education for your child.

- You believe that the greatest educational benefit to your child will be accomplished through the joint efforts of the home and school.

- It is your intent to work cooperatively with the school in every way you can.

You may not always directly convey each of these points to school personnel. Instead, I suggest that they comprise a general position which you intellectually adopt so that it permeates all your interactions as you pursue specific objectives with school staff.

Because nonverbal messages and underlying attitudes are sometimes easier to hear than words, it is important that you always be sincere and honest in your dealings with school personnel. Your interactions will admittedly have a manipulative effect upon the school setting. This in fact is their purpose. However, this effect can be best accomplished through an open and honest interactive process.

You must further frequently remind yourself that operating a public school is a difficult enterprise, and that teaching several subjects for six hours a day to thirty youngsters who are at multiple stages of development is truly a difficult task. Your increased familiarity with the school will quickly convince you of the validity of this statement and will help you maintain your own persistent patience, or perhaps we should say patient persistence, in a positive mode.

Below we'll consider five categories of interactions you may have with school personnel: information-sharing conferences, problem-solving conferences, volunteer activities, special occasions, and incidental contacts. Each has its unique characteristics and opportunities for building and maintaining positive relationships.

Information-Sharing Conferences

Some conferences at school between parents and educators are scheduled and have as their primary purpose the sharing of information. The agenda is usually set by whichever party calls the meeting. The most familiar example of these is the parent-teacher conference typically held at the end of the first quarter of school through which the teacher aims to share information about a student's educational program and performance.

I suggest in Chapter 6 a number of reasons why you may decide not to participate in the regularly scheduled parent-teacher conferences. In the interest of positive relations, however, do attend such conferences if you sense that your attendance is considered important by the teacher. She, or your child's school, may be attempting to reach one hundred percent parent participation in fall conferences; the teacher may want to show off collective student art work or science projects; she may want to introduce you to a few other parents with innovative ideas about a class project.

If you do attend this quarter's end conference, do not attempt to turn it into a problem-solving meeting. Such a meeting requires more than the fifteen or twenty minutes available and a considerable amount of preplanning, as explained in Chapter 7. (Also check Chapter 6 regarding the drawbacks of using this conference as a means of monitoring academic progress.) In general, let the teacher lead. She called the meeting, the agenda is hers. Do ask questions as appropriate, but follow the flow of the conference as laid out by the teacher.

A second type of information-sharing conference occurs when *you* call a meeting with your child's teacher or other school staff to get acquainted, to provide information to them about your child, or to gather information from them. When you initiate a meeting for the purpose of gathering information, follow these guidelines:

1. Let school staff know in advance what information you will be seeking. This will enable them to be prepared for the meeting and avoid what could become annoying delays and/or embarrassment.

2. Always ask questions in a friendly or neutral manner, with no accusatory tone in your voice.

For example, the question "Do I understand correctly that no staff are available for playground supervision before school begins each morning?" will be received differently than "Are you telling me that not a single adult is supervising the playground in the mornings?"

3. If you will be seeking different perspectives on the same issue, always advise a primary source (typically your child's teacher) that you are going to seek the same information from others so that you might better understand the situation. Your actions could otherwise be interpreted as a lack of faith in the answers you were provided by the primary source.

4. If the school employee you are meeting with does not have the information you seek or does not appear willing to share such information, ask with whom you should next visit in order to get this information rather than pressing harder for what you consider to be an appropriate response.

These suggestions will help you get the information you want in an efficient and friendly manner, and information is crucial to your success as an interactive parent. See Chapter 7 for further recommendations on information gathering as part of the problem-solving process.

Problem-Solving Conferences

As with information sharing, two types of problem-solving conferences exist, depending upon whether the meeting is called by school staff or by you. In the former case, the staff will have determined that your child is creating a problem for the school. Perhaps she is not meeting the school's expectations for her rate of learning or classroom behavior. On the other hand, when the school is not meeting *your* expectations, a problem of a different sort exists.

Chapter 7 details interactive problem-solving strategies; however, here we will consider ways to ensure that this form of interaction enables you to maintain positive relations. Let's consider four recommendations:

1. Try not to blend an information-gathering session with a problem-solving session. Educators are busy people, tempted sometimes to speed up the problem-solving process. They may lay out for you in an authoritative manner the nature of the problem and present a solution they believe will work. They then will solicit your agreement with their proposed course of action. In a rushed conference that deals with both information sharing and problem solving, it is easy for parents to get swept away into "solutions" that they may later not endorse. Your resultant dissatisfaction can easily lead to a damaged relationship. If you feel pressed to accept a recommendation that you are uneasy about, do not hesitate to make a friendly retreat for more information gathering and/or further contemplation. If school officials originally called the conference, however, be willing to make a commitment to another meeting within a few days.

2. Consider asking a number of staff members for ideas about how to solve a particular problem. Different individuals may provide you with perspectives and alternatives which you would not have otherwise identified. When appropriate, blend various proposed solutions and give credit freely to the sources of suggestions.

3. If you initiate a problem-solving conference, have a clear idea of what you want to accomplish. Study the information you've gathered and give the problem enough thought ahead of time to offer at least one possible solution. However, be open to other solutions you feel could satisfactorily solve the problem and which may in fact either do so in a less costly or more effective manner.

4. Use appropriate procedures that exist in your child's school for solving problems. For example, schools operate with a recognized chain-of-command and both formal and informal means for

dealing with parent complaints. Learn proper procedures and use them effectively, while not letting them limit you. (See Chapter 7 for more details.)

5. Once a problem has been solved, thank all those who contributed to its solution. Let them know you appreciate their special concerns about your child and their ongoing willingness to work with you.

Volunteer Activities

Schools today are becoming increasingly open to parent volunteers in all aspects of school operations—including the classroom instructional program. Serving as a volunteer provides the interactive parent the opportunity to accomplish a wide number of objectives ranging from positive relations building to observing next year's teacher candidates. You will likely find that you can volunteer for a specific assignment at a regular time each day or week, can participate in special projects of a defined duration, or can be on call for special needs. In order to assure that such volunteer time will result in positive relations with school personnel, follow these recommendations:

1. Make sure that both you and the teacher or principal agree on the commitments you are making, and always keep those commitments. As a regular volunteer, you can quickly become an integral part of a classroom instructional program. The teacher will plan on your presence when designing lessons and student activities. Your unanticipated absence can quickly lead to frustration on the teacher's part. A possible solution to this problem might be for you and another parent to job-share a volunteer slot, thus making the commitment that the teacher can always count on one of you to be there as planned.

2. Always ask what is expected of you as a volunteer. Having a clear understanding of your role and responsibilities will help everyone work together in a comfortable and effective manner.

3. Be careful about "sharing tales out of school." The information you gather as a volunteer can help you in a wide array of your activities as an interactive parent. However, being perceived as a spy or a snitch will quickly eliminate all advantages gained.

None of these comments is intended to suggest that volunteer work with young children cannot be its own best reward. Opportunities exist to help at school in ways far removed from your child's actual classroom or grade level. But many interactive parents want to feel as directly involved with their own child's education as possible, and volunteering in their child's classroom provides a unique opportunity to do just that.

Special Occasions

Certain interactions with school personnel can best be categorized as special occasions. These interactions may consist of visits, phone calls, or written communications, and have as a primary ingredient the development of positive relations. Let's look at some examples:

1. If you have not met your child's teachers or other school staff with whom your child will relate or does relate, be certain to have a short get-acquainted session with each of them. Deliver the general message described on page fifteen relative to your interest in your child's education, share aspects of your home life that relate to your child and his interests and learning, and attempt to learn more about this important individual in your child's life. Resist too much information gathering at this time. Instead, help make school personnel feel good about you as the parent of one of their charges. If you have not accomplished this task previous to reading this book, it should be one of the first steps you take on the road to becoming an interactive parent.

2. A second excellent time for positive interaction with a staff member is shortly after that person has done something that pleases you or your child. Send a note to school with your child, or make a phone call. If you plan to call and your message is directed at the principal, call during the day; if directed at a teacher or librarian, call at home during the evening. Remember that the principal probably deals with several hundred students and parents. It is therefore considerate to remind her of who you are (your name, child's name, and teacher's name). Tell the principal how much you appreciate a given effort, or support a particular decision or action, or how much your child enjoyed a given activity. The same messages are equally appropriate for other school personnel. Most contact these people have with parents involve either problem solving or complaints. A small amount of appreciation will be received as a large reward indeed and will pay like dividends to you and your child.

3. Most adults like to be remembered on significant occasions in their lives—birthdays, Christmas, during an illness—or perhaps on the first sunny day of spring! Have your child take some small item to the teacher on such days. Something homemade would be fine, especially if your child participated in the project. Such a gift can be a gesture of genuine appreciation for the extra effort the teacher is making toward educating your child and can stimulate positive feelings about your child.

4. You may also wish to consider purchasing something special for your child's classroom that can contribute to the educational program. A terrarium, an indoor/outdoor thermometer, or a magazine subscription are examples. Be sure to check with the teacher before doing this, however, to make

certain that the gift would be appropriate. You may also find unique ways to support the curriculum. If, for example, the class is studying birds and you happen to raise chickens, you can offer to bring one to class or invite the class to plan a field trip to visit your chicken farm. Teachers are usually most grateful for such contributions.

Incidental Contact

In many communities parents have incidental contact with school personnel at a grocery store, church, ball game, club meeting, or such. When these chance meetings occur, acknowledge the person with a friendly greeting and, if something comes to mind, make a brief and positive comment about some recent occurrence at school. Do not attempt to turn the incidental contact into an information-gathering or problem-solving conference! After an exhausting day or week neither the principal nor teacher will wish to prolong a brief visit to the supermarket with a parent conference or spend a social evening discussing school policy, but either would happily welcome a friendly compliment. Also, remember that discussing your child's school life in a public place within earshot of others may not be fair to your child and, further, may make the person to whom you're talking uncomfortable. In fact, certified teachers would be breaking a standard professional code of ethics by discussing a child's school life amidst the public. Therefore, you'd be wise to not expect them to do so.

You now recognize five categories of interaction with school personnel and have guidelines for fostering positive relations in each. You are also aware of a more general framework within which to pursue your interactions and can identify those individuals who are likely to have the greatest impact on your child's education.

To help you *maintain* the positive relationships that you develop with school staff, let's look at three final tips:

1. Avoid saying anything negative about the school program, teachers, or administration in front of your child. Such comments will readily be shared

with classmates and may soon find their way to the educator's desk. Though their content may be accurate, negative comments will not help your child adjust to the imperfect setting that comprises the public school system. They can also quickly destroy needed positive relationships. Avoiding negative comments does not mean you won't take your child's side when problems come up, but that you'll try to discuss with your child the *problem*, not the school staff. (Admittedly, sometimes the staff *is* the problem.)

2. Be careful in talking with other parents about your frustrations with your child's school. This information can also find its way into the school hallways, and you may lose the positive image you are trying to establish.

3. If you truly want to help your child, do not lead the parade of educational reform, or play an active role in any movement that could be perceived as an attack on the school or its personnel. You can build positive relations by championing *some* needs of the school—for example, the need for more computers or new science books. However, I must advise you against publicly seeking improved computer or science instruction.

One additional note here, however: During recent years, due to increased public pressure, school staffs have become aware of their need to involve parents more actively in goal setting and program planning. In some states such activities have recently been mandated by statute. When invited as a member of the general parent population to such sessions, privately explore the issues to be discussed with other parents, generate ideas and identify points of agreement, and then jointly attend the meetings. Sometimes these public sessions can redirect entire segments of a school's program in ways that could improve your child's education and that of all his schoolmates.

In other words, the above tips are *not* intended to suggest that an interactive parent should never engage the system in an active way, should not challenge school personnel or policies, or should avoid providing solicited input related to planned structural changes in school programs. I simply want you to be able to engage the system and—for the sake of your child—win! A positive relationship with school personnel is a necessary ingredient for this to happen.

3

Selecting Your Child's Teacher

In his book *Teacher and Child*, educator Haim Ginott presented what he called "a frightening conclusion":

> As a teacher I possess tremendous power to make a child's life miserable or joyous. I can be a tool of torture or an instrument of inspiration. I can humiliate or humor, hurt or heal. In all situations it is my response that decides whether a crisis will be escalated or de-escalated, and a child humanized or de-humanized.

Teachers, parents and administrators all need to remember the profundity of this statement. A poor teacher can literally stunt a child's intellectual and emotional growth and permanently damage a child's interest in learning. An excellent teacher can stimulate academic and emotional growth and inspire lasting enthusiasm for learning. As an interactive parent your greatest responsibility is ensuring that your child is never assigned to a teacher who will subject him to the former, but is assigned to teachers who will offer him large doses of the latter. Many parents ensure that a child sees the best dentist in town, or the best doctor, and some thoroughly interview a potential Friday night baby-sitter. Yet each year many parents allow someone else, sometimes a complete stranger, to chose the persons with whom their children will spend several hours a day, five days a week, nine months of the year. In other words, many parents—most parents!—opt not to be involved in the selection of these frighteningly influential people, their children's teachers. Have you been one of these parents? You don't need to be—you shouldn't be.

In this chapter we'll look at how to identify a school's official and unofficial policies governing the assignment of students to teachers, how to use secondary information in screening potential teachers for your child, and how to evaluate a teacher's instructional capabilities through your own observations. You'll learn how to directly influence the assignment of your child to the classroom you want. We'll assume throughout this chapter that your child attends a school in which he spends the majority of the day with one teacher and in which two or more teachers are available at a given grade level.

You need to realize from the outset that regardless of what policies exist in your child's school relative to assigning children to classrooms, and regardless of anything you may initially be told by school officials, you *can* influence the placement of your child with a desired teacher. Most principals, who have neither the time nor inclination to engage in disputes with interactive parents, will either openly or covertly give in to your request. Even when class assignments are supposedly made on a random basis, perhaps by drawing names from a hat, it is often the principal and school secretary who perform this not-always-so-random process. Further, incompetent teachers hope not to have assigned to them the children of interactive parents, or even of potentially interactive parents. With effective techniques you can accomplish the goal of having your child placed each year with the best teacher available at a given grade level. I have organized these techniques into four distinct steps.

Step One: Determining Policy and Procedure

Your purpose in this first step is to determine who will actually make the decision to place your child in a given classroom and the criteria that will be used to make this decision. Unless you are a friend of the principal, I suggest that you look to the school secretary as your first source of information, particularly if she has occupied her post for several years. As stated in Chapter 2, the school secretary is actually a mid-level manager who often wields considerable power in the system.

When approaching the secretary, try to find a moment when she's alone because she may be reluctant to share this information too publicly. Generally, schools like to guard their right to place children in classrooms according to staff wishes. Also, you'll need to appropriately frame your comments and questions. For example, you could acknowledge that teachers vary in their approaches to teaching, class discipline, etc., and indicate that you are interested in finding *an appropriate match between a teacher and your child*. This is a phrase educators themselves use, and heed, and is preferable to your stating that you want to make certain that your child is placed with the *best* teacher or is *not* assigned to a particular teacher. Ask the secretary how decisions on student placement are made and by whom, when they will be made, and when the decisions will be reported to parents. Wear a warm smile, and remember that you are probably interacting with an individual who can be an important ally or adversary to your cause. You will likely be advised that your child's school addresses the problem of student assignment to teachers in one of three ways:

A stated policy that specifically encourages or allows parental input

Some schools officially recognize that parents may wish to participate in the process of assigning a child to a given teacher. This fact may or may not be well advertised, however, because such openness to parent input can create disturbing problems for the school. Some teachers, for example, may consistently receive a greater number of requests than their "fair share" of the students, while others embarrassingly receive absolutely no requests. However, involving parents in the assignment procedure also has possible advantages for school administrators—it helps them identify any interactive parents and facilitates the placement of their children in the best classrooms, which, in turn, decreases the likelihood of future parent-principal conflict.

A stated policy that students will be placed by the "experts"

Often this type of policy indicates that children will be placed "in accordance with their individual educational needs in a manner that will optimize their academic achievement," which really means that students will be placed in accordance with the values and needs of school personnel. For example, a potentially rowdy child will typically not be placed in the room of a teacher who is a poor disciplinarian; the child of a school board member or fellow teacher will likely be placed in the best available classroom. Some schools favor an even blend of boys and girls or a mix of perceived bright, average and slow students in each classroom. Others allow similar students to be grouped together. Of course, student placement under such a policy may truly be approached with the best interests of specific children in mind. However, such a policy does allow school personnel the freedom to meet the needs of the institution and of specific staff members—needs which sometimes conflict with the educational interests of children.

No stated and/or adhered to policy governing the placement of students, but established procedures with historical precedent

Some districts do not have any official policy or regulation that governs student placement. Nevertheless, usually a common procedure will have emerged. Students may be assigned by the school secretary or principal, by the teachers who will be receiving the students the following fall, by the teachers who are sending a group on to the next grade level, or by lottery. These practices can even vary among different schools within the same school district, and because no policies are involved, are usually the easiest placement procedures for parents to influence.

Once you have the school secretary's description of the process used in your child's school, you need to confirm this information through at least one additional contact. Your selection of which person to consult should be made on the basis of who you now believe makes the decision. If it is reported to be done by teachers, select the one with whom you have the best relationship and make further inquiry. If the principal appears to play the major role, it is best to confirm the procedure directly with him.

If in your inquiry you are told that parents cannot influence the placement of their children in any way, do not be discouraged. The rules of the game then simply become more complicated. You need to understand that there are few firm *no's* in any bureaucracy. If your informant cites formal policy as the reason why you cannot select a teacher, you will need to review a copy of this policy. If you are dealing with the principal at this point, though, it may not be wise to ask immediately for a copy of the policy, for it may simply not exist. You can ask if there is an actual written policy or if what is being referred to is an unofficial policy. If it is written, you can later secure a copy of the policy manual. You will find a copy of the school district policy manual in the school library, public library, or school district office. If necessary, ask the school secretary for a copy of the pertinent pages. She will probably report your request to the principal, but if this is done a few days after discussing the placement matter with him it may not appear as a direct questioning of his knowledge and authority.

At the completion of Step One, you will have a clear understanding of the rules by which your child will be assigned to a teacher. These rules prescribe the information that will be most helpful in influencing this decision, when such information needs to be provided, and to whom it can best be presented. Remember that it is not only in your child's best interest to be placed with an excellent teacher, it is also in both the principal's interest and that of any average to poor teacher to whom your child might otherwise be assigned. Your role as an interactive parent is simply that of helping everyone understand this.

Step Two: Using Other People's Opinions For Teacher Screening

Residents of any given neighborhood or community can frequently identify the local school's best, and worst, teacher. While community opinion about teachers may not always be based on behaviors which are actually valid indicators of teaching effectiveness, overwhelming opinion is usually well grounded. I recommend that you do, in fact, use other people's opinions as a screening device for narrowing the number of potential candidates for selection as your child's teacher.

The sources of information within a community are almost limitless. However, use the following five guidelines as a means of evaluating what you hear:

1. Assess what actual experience the individual has had with the teacher in question. Has it been as the parent of a child in the teacher's classroom, as a neighbor, as a fellow member of an organization? The more removed from actual experience within the educational arena, the less valuable the information is likely to be.

2. Ask each information source to clarify any general statements made. For example, if someone tells you that "Ms. X is a fine teacher," ask the person in what way Ms. X exhibits fine teaching. Try to translate both positive and negative comments into specific reasons and behaviors. There is obviously a considerable difference in value to you in hearing responses such as "Well, he's been at the school a long time. He must be good." or, on the other hand, "My child hated his third grade year with Ms. Y. She shouted at the children and would never provide individual help to students."

3. Disregard information about a teacher that obviously has nothing to do with the teacher's classroom performance. It is unwise, for instance, to use bridge club gossip about a teacher's social life as a basis for judging his teaching. Such information can tell you something about the value system of the speaker, but not about the teacher's effectiveness.

4. You may wish to query the school secretary or other school personnel for additional information. A brief visit with the school principal at this point may be appropriate, or the school nurse, librarian, or counselor. If your child has a particular need—if,

for example, he is a weak reader or requires a well-structured disciplinary situation—you should ask how each teacher teaches reading, helps weak readers, or manages the classroom. Particular strengths can also be mentioned, such as a child's interest in art or creative writing.

5. Many school staff have children of their own who are presently in the school system or who have recently passed through it. Find out which classrooms school employees had their own children assigned to at different grade levels. Include also in this review the children of school board members and influential people in your community—all of whom are often catered to by school personnel.

Other people's opinions can be important as you select a teacher for your child for a given school year. Gathering these opinions should be a planned, not random, process, focusing on the specific rather than general, and should be thorough, not slight.

Step Three: Classroom Observation

One of the best ways to evaluate someone in a job is to actually see him perform. This is not often possible in actual employee selection, but it is possible in selecting a teacher for your child.

Me, you may ask, evaluate a teacher by actually going into the classroom and observing the teacher in action? Would the school allow me to do this? Could I actually gather valid information? The answer to all three questions is *yes*. Below, you'll find a number of insights into this third stage of selecting a teacher for your child—classroom observation.

First, it is possible that the information you gathered during the previous stage will make this step unnecessary. For example, there may be only three teachers available at a given grade level and one of them may be considered by everyone in your community to be the finest teacher in the entire school. Nevertheless, seeing for yourself how a given teacher teaches, and how the children respond, is probably the most reliable means of selecting the best teacher for your child.

Now, before looking at specific observation steps to follow, you need to become a little familiar with the principles of effective teaching. Prior to 1975, it would have been impossible to provide you with much guidance in this regard that was not based almost entirely upon "expert opinion," much of which has since been demonstrated to have been incorrect. During the last two decades, however, researchers have begun to identify effective teacher behaviors and teaching methods which do affect student learning. Below is a summary.

Management Skills

Studies have demonstrated that as little as fifty percent of the time allocated to public school attendance is actually used for instruction. Student absences, assemblies, opening exercises, class changes, and lunch periods account for twenty-one percent of the school day. Another sixteen percent is lost in the classroom itself—time devoted to organizing the class, changing instructional groups, managing student behavior, and so on. The above amounts of lost instructional time are averages, and vary considerably by teacher. In addition, not all students are fully engaged in learning during all of the three or so hours of actual daily instruction. Student *engaged time* can be less than three hours.

What you need to know here is that a consistent relationship exists between how much students learn and the actual amount of time students devote to learning. A teacher's ability to maximize student learning time has been termed *management skill*. This phrase refers to the ability to keep the class moving smoothly through the instructional day with a minimum of interruption from disciplining students, waiting in line, transitioning from activity to activity, or wandering away from a lesson's objectives. Another management skill involves the use of a system, and perhaps rules, that enable students to attend to procedural and personal needs (such as getting necessary materials or going to the bathroom) without interrupting the teacher or the flow of instruction.

Clearly-Established Learning Objectives

The effective use of time requires that a given lesson be organized around clearly-stated lesson objectives. An effective teacher knows what the objectives are, shares them with students early in the lesson, designs a learning environment that stimulates student participation in meaningful learning activities, and frequently monitors student performance to see if the intended objectives are being met.

Physical Involvement In Teaching

An effective teacher is physically involved in the process of teaching. He provides a variety of learning activities, actively exchanges information, and engages, excites, monitors, and assists students. The effective teacher frequently moves around the room, checking on students' progress, letting them know he knows what they are doing and is interested in their learning. The pace is brisk; the atmosphere is lively. Learning steps may be kept small, with students moving quickly from step to step, or whole processes may be explored, attempted, analyzed, and practiced. Effective teachers are able to manage multiple activities simultaneously and to do it all with a smile.

A Level of Instruction Appropriate to Each Learner

Activities should be designed to meet the varied learning needs and levels of the students. Violation of this important principle leads to student frustration, time away from task, and discipline problems. Learning activities also need to allow for high levels of learner success—a minimal rate of seventy-five percent when teacher assistance is available and nearly one hundred percent during independent practice.

Individualized Student Interaction

Positive learner gains are associated with some variety of ongoing recognition of each student by the teacher. By frequently moving among pupils, as noted above, for example, the teacher can be in continual contact with individual students, allow reasonably equitable time for each, and continuously monitor individual progress. Studies show that students gain the most in classrooms in which a great deal of direct, interactive instruction occurs.

Teacher Expectations

Studies have consistently demonstrated that teacher expectations can have tremendous influence on student learning. As with self-fulfilling prophesies, if a teacher believes a student is capable of academic success, the student is successful. Likewise, unfortunately, low expectations produce the predicted effect.

Effective teachers know what it is that they want their students to learn and are convinced that students can learn it. These teachers set high goals and optimistically convey high expectations for all students, as opposed to only subsets of students. Then they monitor student needs closely so they can creatively find ways to help students meet the expectations.

An Absence of Negative Behavior Directed Toward Students

Research findings have consistently noted a negative relationship between student learning gains and any teacher behavior which belittles, embarrasses, harasses, or generally downgrades students. Teacher mistrust of students also negatively affects student academic achievement.

The above introduction to the research-based qualities of effective teaching is admittedly brief. Nevertheless, it provides a baseline for observing a teacher and reaching conclusions regarding the teacher's suitability for your child. Appendix A contains further information that will help you organize your classroom observations.

Currently, an additional set of research-based criteria is emerging which is expanding our definition of and enabling our identification of the truly excellent teacher. Some of these criteria elaborate on the above principles and some suggest new directions supported by such diverse areas of study as brain research and futuring. A few examples follow:

• Students learn best when new material is connected to prior knowledge and other subject areas. Some teachers no longer teach math from 9:00 to 9:45, reading from 9:45 to 10:30, etc., but rather blend several subject areas in a series of interrelated learning activities, often brought together under a single theme. These teachers also introduce new information only in relationship to existing knowledge.

• The role of a teacher as the presenter of knowledge is being replaced with teacher as planner, facilitator, and coach. A classroom in which every student is completely engaged in learning—singly, in pairs, in small groups—while the teacher moves among them checking a student's progress in one corner, then giving hints to another child, next questioning a group in the library area—suggests a master designer who can work magic with her students. A teacher using much of the class period to explain a lesson in lecture format while students sit passively unengaged presents an old, ineffectual model of teaching to which far too many practitioners still cling.

• Our new economic world and the dawning of the Information Age demand that students become thinkers—hypothesizing, analyzing, synthesizing, evaluating, and innovating. Thus the teacher who emphasizes rote memory and regurgitation of facts is a teacher who is not growing with his profession. Excellent teachers ask open-ended questions of their students rather than seek single, correct answers; they foster inquiry and experimentation; they assess student learning in ways that tap students' depth of understanding.

• Excellent teachers assume responsibility for student success and continuously alter teaching methods and learning activities in an attempt to enable all students to succeed. If a teacher focuses on a textbook and on making sure that all of the material in it is covered through a series of lectures, readings, and end-of-the-chapter exercises and tests—you can be confident that twenty-five percent to fifty percent of the students will not master the curriculum and that at least seventy-five percent will forget within a year whatever they supposedly learned.

The classrooms you will observe may look very different from those which you attended twenty to thirty years ago. In fact the closer the similarity the more suspicious you should be. Young students learn language, for example, by actively engaging others in conversation, not by sitting in straight rows silently completing worksheets; they learn measurement skills most readily by pouring half-cups of rice into whole cup containers or determining how tall a classmate is with a measuring tape, not reading a textbook assignment. Excellent teachers do indeed create magic—an entire classroom of young people enthusiastically engaged in the learning process. You want your child to get as much of this magic as possible.

As you build your commitment to making classroom observations and begin the practice of interactive parenting, you will probably want to review the above research summary and Appendix A many times. If your courage wanes as you prepare to be an observer, remember that you will be visiting a *public* school, funded by state and local taxes, existing for the purpose of educating the children of your community. School officials cannot legally deny you access to the school for observation purposes. Remember, and remind others if necessary, that you are not evaluating the teachers you observe, but are attempting to find a teacher you feel will be particularly appropriate for your child.

I recommend the following six steps for carrying out classroom observations:

1. Arrange for an initial classroom observation through the principal's office. State that you are very interested in your child's education, that you are looking for a good match between your child and a teacher, and that you want an opportunity to consider what classroom your child might be placed in for the following school year. You may be told that any time is acceptable, and that you can simply check in at the office or call a day or two in advance. Do request that the teacher(s) involved

be advised of your intentions. If you are discouraged from making observations, politely persist. If you are denied access to a classroom, I refer you to Chapter 7, particularly the section on use of the chain-of-command.

2. Before the observation day, call the teacher at school or send her a note to confirm the arrangements. Always remember that few parents ever observe a teacher in the classroom; further, that few observations are ever made by anyone, including the principal. A teacher will thus wonder what your motives are, and may feel uneasy with you in his room. A brief conversation or note may allay these fears.

3. Time your observation so that you are present during at least one complete lesson or activity period and the beginning of a second. The beginning of the day may be an ideal time because you may be able to visit with the teacher briefly before the instructional day begins.

4. Attempt to locate yourself unobtrusively at the side or rear of the room. The children will soon forget that you are there, and normal behavior will ensue.

5. Observe carefully what occurs. Let Appendix A be your guide. Take brief descriptive notes, then soon after the visit, refer to Appendix A to complete a detailed observation record.

6. When leaving the classroom, smile a thank you or quietly place a note on the teacher's desk thanking him for the opportunity to visit his classroom.

After completing both informal information gathering and classroom observations you will probably find it quite easy to reach a decision about which teacher you want your child assigned to for the upcoming academic year. If you should find that two teachers are equally desirable, your task in Step Four will be easier. On the other hand, if your answer to the hypothetical multiple-choice question is a definite "none-of-the-above," I refer you to Chapter 8 for a consideration of alternatives.

Step Four: Securing the Desired Placement

Your next project is interacting with the system in order to arrange the placement of your child with the teacher you've selected. Follow these five steps:

1. Make an appointment to see the teacher you have selected. Explain to her your interest in your child's education and state that you want to support the efforts of your child's teacher in every possible way. Explain to the teacher that you feel she is a fine teacher and that you want to make certain your child is assigned to her classroom for the next school year. Having offered a genuine compliment to the teacher and stated your intentions, you will likely secure her support.

2. Make an appointment with the principal. Discuss your strong interest in your child's education and in your desire to enter a partnership with the school regarding your child's educational program. Indicate that you wish to have your child placed with the teacher you've selected. Make certain that the principal understands that you are quite committed to this placement and attempt to secure a commitment from him to the same effect. If such a commitment is made, follow up the meeting with a dated written note to the principal confirming your understanding. Keep a copy of this communication.

3. A principal's failure to make such a commitment suggests a number of possibilities: that he does not understand the extent to which it is to his advantage to make this placement, that he may feel pushed by you and does not wish to give in, or that he does not have the power to place your child with the teacher of your choice. The first two

possibilities can frequently be dealt with simply through a direct but pleasant restatement of your position. A principal will sometimes advise you that he cannot officially guarantee your desired assignment, but that he will give your request careful consideration. This tends to be a way of informing you not to worry, but to remain quiet about the unspoken understanding between the two of you.

4. If the principal claims not to have the authority or power to make such a placement, you are likely dealing with either a matter of policy or a situation in which a committee of teachers makes the assignments. Ask which is the case, and then ask for his assistance in the matter. You may need to review any written policies involved, or to talk with whoever is in a position to affect the decision. Be assured, however, that the principal can probably bring about the desired result.

5. If you encounter difficulties, schedule another conference and retreat to rethink your position. You may wish to take your spouse or another interested party to the next conference. This display of strength suggests your seriousness. If necessary, point out rather directly that you truly believe it to be in the interests of not only your child, but of the principal as well to have your child placed with the selected teacher. Utilize any stated procedures or policies that may be supportive; ignore such if they are not helpful. Cite any precedent that you may be aware of from previous years. Each situation is different—each set of procedures, each principal, each parent.

Most typically few difficulties will be encountered. School personnel are in the business of pleasing people and hence in keeping the institution running smoothly. In fact, for many administrators this is of paramount importance. Your efforts will almost always be rewarded, and you will have secured for your child for an entire school year the highest quality educational experience available at that place and time. You may also have avoided a terrible experience for your child—one that could have affected your child's learning, and life, for many years.

No other act as an interactive parent is as important as selecting your child's teacher. Through carefully planned interactions with school officials you can accomplish this goal—providing both you and your child a meaningful and enjoyable school year.

4

Choosing Your Child's Curriculum

Deciding which body of knowledge—subjects, skills, concepts, processes—schools should teach has been an ongoing problem for educators...for a very long time.

> There are doubts concerning the business [of education] since all people do not agree in those things which they would have a child taught, both with respect to improvement in virtue and a happy life; nor is it clear whether the object of it should be to improve the reason or rectify the morals. From the present mode of education we cannot determine with certainty to which men incline, whether to instruct a child in what will be useful to him in life, or what tends to virtue, or what is excellent; for all these things have their separate defenders.
>
> — Aristotle, 300 B.C.ca

Within the American public school system, Aristotle's debate continues, as the curriculum swings from trend to trend—return to the basics, life adjustment, vocational training, sex education, intensive phonics, the new basics, new math, and so on. In many districts we still "cannot determine with certainty to which men incline...." Whatever the current trends, each of our nation's schools does teach a curriculum—a collection of subjects and related skills, concepts, and processes, to its students. However, as an interactive parent you can determine and, in part, create your own child's curriculum. The school does have curriculums to which your child will be exposed, curriculums we will discuss below; however, it is important that you not leave the task (and privilege) of determining your child's curriculum entirely up to the school.

As you begin to think about curriculum, you'll find it helpful to draw an underlying distinction between "schooling" and "educating." *Schooling* refers to formal schooling processes and learning activities more or less presented to your child simply by virtue of her attendance at school. Most parents presume schooling equates to educating; that is, that their child is being educated *because* he is being schooled. However, since public schooling, if looked at closely, always includes some things you don't want your child to learn and omits other things you do want her to learn, and also involves varying degrees of schooling success, you have to ask whether educating—as defined by you—occurs or not. Your definition of "education" will be comprised of the knowledge, skills, and attitudes that *you* want your child to develop by the time she completes her schooling and joins the adult world.

Most parents unquestioningly allow public schools to both school and educate their children. As an interactive parent, however, you can accept the responsibility of seeing that your children are, by your own definition, educated, viewing the school as a tool that you have consciously selected to help you. You'll need first to recognize that *education* involves more than one curriculum: it involves an out-of-school curriculum, which we'll address later, and four in-school curriculums. Let's look at those in-school curriculums now.

The Four Curriculums of the Public School

To educators, the term "curriculum" means the **official curriculum**. An official curriculum is one that has been adopted by the school board and exists in written form, typically in a big notebook called "The Curriculum Guide." Usually school staff themselves have written the guide, and from time to time they change or update it. However, knowing how staff wrote the guide gives us clues to its appropriateness for the students of the school. If the staff considered what the world may be like in twenty to forty years, studied the local setting and the students of their school, gathered public input on desirable outcomes of the educational process, and then wrote a curriculum especially suited to their local students, chances are that the curriculum is a good one for their school. A curriculum for an inner city school, for instance, would include skills and concepts related to city life. A curriculum for a predominantly Native American school would include skills and concepts related to the cultural heritage of its students. If, on the other hand, and much more typically, the staff referred to a textbook series in each subject area and used the publisher's roster of learning goals and objectives to write the guide—goals and objectives written with no awareness of or sensitivity to local needs and values—we know the curriculum may not be so well suited to local students. This process further results in a curriculum that is discipline-based— that is defined around science, English, history, and so on—without any recognition of the ways in which all knowledge is interrelated and how the most important things we want children to learn are usually not contained in a textbook. In other words, the appropriateness of a school's official curriculum is colored by how it was written. Also, the "Guide" is often just that, a *guide*, not a mandate. In any one school, some teachers will follow it closely, some will browse through it and teach portions, while other teachers will ignore it entirely and let their textbooks be their guides or develop their own curriculum.

Thus, the official curriculum becomes translated by each teacher into what I call the **classroom curriculum**. Since each class is a microcosm, rarely supervised directly, each teacher is unofficially free to teach whichever portions of the official curriculum he chooses. Sometimes a teacher just doesn't like parts of the guide; sometimes a teacher doesn't know much about a subject, like music, and elects, therefore, to omit it; sometimes a teacher has a passion for one topic, like wildflowers, so teaches it even if it's not in the guide. Now and then, despite the best of plans, he may simply run out of time. In any case, those portions of the official guide and whatever extra topics and skills the teacher decides to teach make up the classroom curriculum.

Beyond these two subject-related curriculums, two other curriculums exist. First, there is an observable, describable **unstated curriculum**. Every school and every teacher exposes students to a value system, often, in fact, imposing it on them. Students may, for example, be urged to be obedient, respectful of adults, accepting of authority, verbally nonabusive, socially nonagressive, nationalistic, environmentally conscious, holiday oriented, and so on. Often these values serve the school and society well; sometimes they don't. We have to ask, for instance, if unwavering acceptance of authority led millions to bow down to Nazism, while at the same time asking how we could possibly have orderly schools and communities without an acceptance of authority. The point here is that we'll find in every class and school an unstated curriculum. It will be manifested in varied ways within a school and be visible, or audible, to us.

Finally, there is a **hidden curriculum** in operation in each school. The hidden curriculum is also in part comprised of values, and of information, but how and when this curriculum is conveyed is not so clear. Instead of being easily observed and described, it is passed from child to child and teacher to child in casual, subtle, unconscious fashion, just by happenstance throughout each school day. When a teacher, for example, punishes a misbehaving student by having him do extra schoolwork, she is unconsciously teaching the student that schoolwork is a punishment. If she does this often enough, the student will surely develop a deep disliking for schoolwork, and perhaps for school. If, for another example, a teacher offers a prize for the best essay, she is indirectly telling the students that essay-writing itself is not necessarily pleasurable and worth doing; its value lay in the prize. Peers also pass along hidden values at school. A child joining in for the first time with a group of kickball players at recess, for example, learns to holler and scoff at his teammates, if that's what the regular players are already doing. If they are treating each other with respect, the newcomer will emulate their behavior and learn to respect his peers. From his peers he will also learn much about friendship, cooperation and competition, the implications of socioeconomic status, drugs, sex, and the value of other humans. As is evident, the hidden curriculum is probably the least controllable and visible of the four curriculums and has more to do with values and social interaction than with academic subject matter.

As you can see from the above discussion, while you may easily ascertain the official curriculum of your child's school, you won't so easily be able to determine the classroom, unstated, and hidden curriculums; yet all four are at work. Knowing this, you can be aware of your need, as an interactive parent, to monitor the effects of all of them, to support and enhance, probably in most cases, what your child is learning from his curriculums, but also to counteract some of what he is learning from them.

As you consider ways of supporting, enhancing, and counteracting, you may benefit from recognizing how the whole issue of curriculum in American schools has developed during the twentieth century and come to understand the kinds of factors that affect your child's, every child's, school curriculum today. Then you will realize just what it is that steers our curriculums in this and that and the other direction, and you'll see the larger, whole picture of what you are supporting, enhancing, or counteracting.

In his 1980 book *The Third Wave*, futurist Alvin Toffler identified what he believed was the underlying, hidden curriculum of mass education in industrialized societies such as ours. Toffler pointed to an invisible curriculum that espouses punctuality, obedience, routinization, and the ability and willingness to do rote, repetitive work. He explained that the larger, societal factor that drove this curriculum was the turn-of-the-century Industrial Revolution which created a tremendous need for assembly-line factory workers. America wanted its schools to produce employees who would show up on time, begin at the sound of the bell, take orders from management, and perform tedious, repetitive tasks. Getting out the product was the goal.

But today we are experiencing an economic revolution of a different sort. The assembly-line model of employment and schools is fast becoming outmoded. Employers are calling for workers who are creative problem solvers, who can work in teams, who can understand social and technological systems. They want workers who can acquire and evaluate data, use computers to process information, and who are committed to lifelong learning. We have a new set of economic and educational buzzwords: twenty-first century, world class standards, advanced technologies, the Information Age, critical thinking, performance-based assessment, and Quality! We are more aware than ever that we are as a society competing for our economic lives on a global scale. American industry is crying for change—within its own walls and within the public schools where workers are produced. In many ways, these stirrings of change are very exciting, at least for the enlightened among educators, and, if education reform has sweeping effects, we could soon create a generation of process-oriented thinkers and problem-solvers attuned to high technologies. If public school education reform fails, we will probably create the new generation of workers outside of public schools, in private and home schools, in business-managed schools, through computer network education, through apprenticeship programs, and through other means we haven't dreamed of yet. Parents will play critical decision-making roles as this drama unfolds.

Choosing Your Child's Curriculum

Today our public schools seem caught between the Industrial Revolution and the demands of the twenty-first century. What you need to recognize is that your child's curriculum is currently, therefore, probably in flux, that it threads in both directions, backwards and forwards. Knowing this will help you sift through the curriculums that you see emerging in your child's education and consciously decide to support and enhance forward-looking curricular focuses and to remain neutral about or counteract backward-looking focuses. If, for example, when you observe two teachers, you see that one is quite regimental while the other encourages choice, exploration, and discussion, you can decide which of the two is likely to provide the kinds of curricular focuses to which you want your child exposed. If, for a second example, your child is being taught that *right* answers (vs. good thinking) win praise, you can counteract by encouraging diverse thinking at home. If, for yet another example, your child is being told to heed and unquestioningly obey all authority figures, you can teach him that authorities can err and that if harm is being done, authority should be questioned.

In cases like these, what you'll be wisely doing, in effect, is determining and delivering your own curriculum to your child. You'll be making that distinction between *schooling* and *educating*. If your child isn't being satisfactorily educated by the schools, *she counts on you*, and I propose that it is your responsibility, to see that changes come about that will ensure that she is being educated, not merely schooled. You have taken on responsibility for her physical well-being, you provide her basic needs, you select dentists and doctors to do what you want done for her health; should you not also take on responsibility for this lifeblood of her future—her education?

One key factor in doing so is to take a close look at those curriculums of which I spoke above and then identify your own curriculum for her education. Begin by envisioning her high school graduation. What do you think she should know and be able to do when she finishes school? What knowledge should she possess? What skills? What kind of thinker should she be? What attitudes and values about learning, work, socializing, and herself should she have? In other words, ask yourself what your aims are for her longterm, even lifelong, education. What will the "exit outcomes" of her education be?

To help you get started, let's look at some examples from recently adopted state vision statements and outcomes-oriented curriculums, school district curriculums, and from an informative book by former public educator Borg Hendrickson titled *How to Write a Low-Cost / No-Cost Curriculum for Your Home-School Child*.

> My child's curriculum year-by-year should enable him or her to:
> - think logically and critically
> - maintain a strong sense of self-worth
> - perceive and strive toward excellence
> - communicate effectively

- value a healthy environment
- demonstrate aesthetic appreciation
- question authority
- understand and use mathematics
- process, interpret and apply information
- live self-reliantly
- know the chronology of American history
- demonstrate creativity
- understand what she reads
- recognize and discuss important social issues
- act as a responsible citizen
- be committed to health and fitness
- accept responsibility for personal actions
- exhibit respect and concern for others
- concentrate and persevere on tasks

Now, how about your own list? Pick and choose from the above statements those that seem to ring true for you and your child. Then add your own. Get input from your child's other parent if possible, and from your child. Remember to think about the longterm: What will she need to know and be able to do when she graduates? Remember that everything she is learning now contributes to longterm outcomes—whether you like it or not. If, for example, you list "self-reliance" as one of your outcomes, she can and should begin learning self-reliance in kindergarten...or earlier. At every grade level, self-reliance training should be a part of her curriculum.

When you have finished writing your list, you will have identified what it is that will constitute *educating* your child. Now let's turn back to *schooling*.

What official curriculum is being used at your child's school? Ask the school secretary where you can review a copy of this curriculum. Then, as you read it, look first for a broad definition of the school's (or school district's) intended outcomes for your child's learning experience. These may be stated in a district-wide mission statement or may be described only in terms of course requirements (four years of English, two years of science). On the other hand, a school may have adopted a more specific set of learner outcomes its faculty and community consider the intended outcomes of major significance. For example, an elementary school curriculum might contain as major outcomes becoming a complex thinker, a self-directed learner, a collaborative worker, a quality producer, and a community contributor. Second, look for the curriculum for your child's grade or level. The curriculum for each grade or level, such as primary, should outline subject area outcomes or objectives.

Make a copy of these parts of the official curriculum for yourself if you can, so you can refer to them throughout the school year. Then begin comparing your own list of what you consider of greatest significance for your child's education with the school's curriculum. Begin to identify those official curricular goals or yearly outcomes that you will want to support and enhance and those you may want to counteract. Identify holes in the official curriculum that you feel you'd like to fill at home.

Next, visit your child's teacher to find out what her classroom curriculum will consist of. Will she devotedly follow the official curriculum? If not, what will she leave out and what will she add? Within each subject area, what will she emphasize and what will she deemphasize or cover only lightly? As you visit with the teacher, try to remain neutral about what she plans to teach, even if you don't always agree that she's making the best choices. You aren't likely to bring about changes in her classroom curriculum and will probably waste time trying. You could also alienate the teacher, which is something you should avoid doing. Remember during your visit that you are just gathering information. Let the teacher know, in fact, that you are planning to continually help your child at home with his education and that you need a clear understanding of what she will be teaching in order to provide that help.

Take your information home. Make further comparisons with your list. You'll now understand much of what your child's schooling will include, what its planned outcomes are, and the ways in which it will contribute towards the education you have planned for your child. (See Figure 1.)

Figure 1

My Child's Curriculum for Grade __		
parent	school	teacher
My child's curriculum will enable him to: 1. 2. 3. 4. 5. .	The official curriculum will enable him to 1. 2. 3. 4. 5. .	The classroom curriculum will enable him to: 1. 2. 3. 4. 5. .

If you find any big holes, look for ways to fill them. If the teacher plans no music program, for example, you could arrange for piano lessons, if piano appeals to your child. Or you could play lots of music on a cassette player at home and discuss with your child the various types of music and instruments and rhythms you hear. If you live by the sea, but your teacher plans no field trips to the seashore as part of her classroom curriculum, you can take your child to the seashore for tidepool explorations. Or find a friendly wildlife biologist who would accompany you to the shore to give your child some informal sea life lessons. You could bring home a collection of findings from the shore, study them, read about them, label them, and go look for more. If environmental awareness will not be a part of your child's classroom curriculum, you can model environmentally sound practices at home. In other words, you can fill in the gaps that you find between the official and classroom curriculums and your own curriculum—your list of outcomes.

By doing this every year as your child progresses up the grades, *you* will remain in control of his curriculum, you will support the positives and counteract the negatives in his public school schooling, you will be responsible for and in charge of his education. You will ensure that he gets educated … that, indeed he gets the best possible education.

Currently many states and school districts are taking steps to redefine school curriculums by establishing new learner outcomes for all students. These outcomes tend to reflect the now recognized need for new skills, abilities and attitudes critical to the future success of our children. Parent involvement in the setting of these new outcomes is critical to the success of educational reform. If you are given the opportunity, your involvement in such an effort can enable you to influence the degree of congruity between your set of desired outcomes and those of the school and the classroom. The more these three sets of outcomes overlap, the more you and your child's teachers can focus on the same learner goals and provide mutual support toward their achievement.

5

Setting Standards

"Quality is Job 1!" declares a well-known Ford Motor Company advertisement. But as our schools suffer attacks from both industry and the public for producing young people who have little sense of quality, who are not only unable to create excellence, but who do not even know what it is, we have to wonder who's doing Job 1.

In Chapter 4 you identified a set of learning outcomes for your child—knowledge, abilities, and attitudes you believe are critical to your child's becoming educated. You of course will want to monitor your child's progress toward achieving these outcomes, and Chapter 6—Monitoring Academic Progress—will help you do so. As a preface to this activity, however, we first must consider the issue of *standards*. The term "standards" refers to criteria that describe quality performance. If we agree that children should communicate effectively as a result of their education, for example, what standard will define success? What will a quality piece of writing look like, or a quality speech sound like? On a more general level, what quality of learning should be acceptable? And meritorious? What standards of quality do schools convey? How high should these standards be?

You can leave the answers to these questions up to the school system if you wish. It does have standards. Most high schools, for example, actually have three standards, the first of which I call the *elite standard*. This standard applies to those students earning high grades who are considered by school staff as the preordained *capable* ones. Teachers establish high standards for these students and convey to them high expectations for success. The second standard is what I call the *extracurricular standard*. In many schools this standard is operationally defined as a 2.0 grade point average and thus eligibility for participation in extracurricular activities, which, incidentally, can lead students towards those classes which most easily yield higher grades and away from more challenging academic work. The third standard in our public high schools is the *graduation standard,* which simply requires a D grade in each class—and leads to a diploma. As I said, you can leave the setting of standards up to the schools, but....

The issue of standards presently dominates the American education scene. In a flurry of activities on both national and state levels, educators are attempting to establish new standards for student learning, quality teaching, and school performance. Parents, the business community, and legislators are among the most interested onlookers and increasingly involved participants. While it is recognized that developing a new definition of what we want our children to know and be able to do is a necessary first step in renewing public education, a twenty-first century curriculum does not in itself speak to the issue of quality—namely, what level of student performance will be judged acceptable, certifiable and praiseworthy. The D-minus diploma and other definitions of "minimum competency" no longer appear to meet the criteria.

The attempt to define a new set of standards is stirring among educators an even greater debate about the very belief systems upon which much of our present education system rests. In one camp are those who believe all children are capable learners and that all but the truly learning handicapped can master the curriculum at a high standard given appropriate instruction and sufficient learning opportunities. Educators in this camp point to the power of expectation, the literature on the multiplicity and fluidity of intelligence, and the benefits of multiple instructional strategies. They also note the outstanding academic performance of a majority of students in some schools whose student bodies consist almost entirely of so-called *disadvantaged, at-risk* children. These educators are concerned about the system's tendency to set low standards, to provide too few alternative paths to learning, and to limit the ways students are allowed to demonstrate curriculum mastery. They believe that *teaching* only occurs when *learning* results—a profound and revolutionary thought. The focus of these educators is inward. They look to each other and to educator-researchers for innovative ways to meet students' needs. They are continuously evaluating and adjusting their educational philosophies, trying out new organizational schema and new instructional strategies, and devising new ways to assess learning—in an effort to adapt to a changing pre-twenty-first century student body, to a changing world. Unfortunately, in many school districts this group comprises a minority of the faculty and administrative staff.

A second camp of educators points the finger of failure at the students and at society—student apathy, television, drugs, learning disabilities, poverty, violence, uninvolved parents. This group defines teaching as the act of presenting information, of providing students with the *opportunity* to learn, of letting students come to the subject rather than of taking the subject to students—a definition of teaching that has dominated education for many years. Many of these educators believe that one of their jobs is separating winners from losers—serving as gatekeepers to college, employment, and the rewards of our economic system. Because this camp sets high standards but conveys low-to-mediocre expectations to most students, only the *deserving* reach the standards, while the majority continue to reach *average*, and an all-too-large number become discouraged, many to the point of dropping out.

Three variables are volleyed between those in the two camps: ability, expectation, and achievement. Your understanding of these concepts and their relationships can lead to profoundly positive changes in your child's education.

Ability

Educators and psychologists usually refer to learning ability as intelligence, or IQ (intelligence quotient). You are probably familiar with this acronym, and like many educators, probably believe that children's learning is considerably influenced by IQ. In reality, however, an IQ test is actually a form of standardized achievement test. The creators of intelligence tests assume that each child has been exposed to the same general learning experiences and then design a test which measures how much each child learned from those experiences. The IQ score is a means of comparing one child's performance with that of children in a norm group, just as is done with other norm-referenced standardized achievement tests. The typical IQ test favors children who grew up exposed to the curriculum provided by the dominant culture. If this curriculum was further enriched by highly interested parents who provided stimulating learning experiences—books, films, travel, discussion—a student's preparation for the IQ achievement test is even greater. Thus IQ testing and the very notion of general intelligence favor students from middle and upper socioeconomic levels, the same students who typically are more successful in public schools.

Further, IQ tests measure only what students know now. They are predictive of what children will learn in the future only if that future is the same as the past—the same experiences, the same home environment, and the same educational milieu. Ample research confirms this statement. Studies have shown, for example, that IQ scores increase as the amount of one's schooling increases, and children who begin school later than their age mates have lower IQs than similar children who have been in school.

While intelligence *tests* no longer play a significant role in most children's educations, the IQ legacy—the belief that ability is innate and fixed, that some children are smart and some are stupid—continues to have a large impact. Many teachers adjust their expectations to what they *perceive to be* a student's abilities—as suggested by intelligence test results, prior grades, physical appearance, personality, social standing, the performance of older siblings, and so on. These expectations are often conveyed to individual students.

Students who believe that their intelligence level is fixed—frequently taking their cues from their teachers—define themselves as good or poor learners and believe that what happens to them in school is a matter of chance, not controlled by their own actions. On the other hand, students who believe that intelligence can be changed also believe that their personal efforts will affect their learning. They view school as a place where they can *get smarter*.

Expectation

Expectation is one of the most powerful factors influencing your child's education. Expectation is often formulated around perceived ability, and perceptions of intelligence have proven to be more powerful predictors of academic achievement than has measured intelligence! Yes, you read that sentence correctly. Research has clearly demonstrated that students' academic achievement, as measured by school grades and even by standardized achievement tests, will conform more closely to teacher expectation levels than to measured intelligence. In other words, as noted in Chapter 3 but worthy of repeating here, if teachers *believe* a student is capable and can succeed, he almost always will succeed. Unfortunately, the opposite is also true. The popular adage that parents and educators rarely get from children more than they expect is now a well-supported educational maxim.

It is important to recognize, incidentally, that "expectations" and "standards" are not the same. Standards identify criteria that define acceptable performance. Criteria for effective written communication thus may include the proper use of writing conventions such as grammar and spelling, the clear expression of ideas, language appropriate to the intended audience, etc. Together such criteria define quality writing. Expectations are a teacher's, parents', or student's own perceptions of the probability that the student will reach the standard.

Teachers can be reluctant to raise either standards or expectations. They worry about students' possible frustration and failure if standards are too high, notwithstanding the fact that if set too low, students will not achieve what they are capable of achieving. And high expectations for student learning place much greater demands on those who convey those expectations. For example, teachers who believe that all children are capable learners whose level of achievement is greatly influenced by the quality of instruction they receive must continuously attempt to improve their own teaching competencies in a perpetual effort to enable every child to successfully master the curriculum. Contrarily, those teachers who set high standards but convey varying levels of expectation feel justified in stimulating student learning that generally conforms to what is called a *normal curve*, in which most students are expected to do *average* work. These teachers further don't expect twenty-five percent or more of their students to learn very much in spite of the teacher's instructional effort, and, unfortunately, these low expectations are almost always met. Some teachers simply lower standards and expectations for everyone in a silently negotiated truce that guarantees minimal effort among all concerned.

Achievement

On a daily, weekly, and quarterly basis, we've traditionally thought of achievement as being reflected by assignment and report card grades, routine quiz and test scores, and so on. We've also viewed yearly grade promotion as a stamp of significant achievement. Further, many have assumed that a student's academic achievement results directly from his ability and from the expectations he holds for his own learning, which we refer to as *motivation*. The task of setting standards for your child requires a reexamination of these conventional beliefs.

A goal of the education system has been the creation of a balance among three variables—ability, expectation, achievement—so that the student could function in a comfortable learning situation. The following examples, based upon the traditional viewpoint, will help you understand this concept of balance.

High Ability—High Expectation—High Achievement

The student, parents, and teacher are usually pleased in this situation. The child is living up to the expectations of parents and teachers, and probably his own, and is using his talents well. (And the teacher is lauded for her good teaching.)

Average Ability—Average Expectation—High Achievement

This imbalance appears paradoxical. A child in this situation has traditionally been referred to by educators as an "overachiever," said to be making the very best of his abilities and demonstrating an unusual amount of motivation (and, again, the teacher, too, is praised).

Low Ability—High Expectation—Low Achievement

In this model one party, often the parent, is said to be conveying unreasonable expectations. The low achievement is seen by educators as in keeping with the student's natural ability and the concomitant notion that intelligence is fixed.

The balance formula represented by these examples has served educators well for many years. If a child learns readily in the system as traditionally designed—with its emphasis on verbal skills, step-by-step methodologies, rote memorization, etc.—the student is viewed as intelligent and responsive to high expectations (and quality teaching of course). If the child is less successful as a learner, he often is thought to have average ability or perhaps parents whose expectations are low (and the teacher is making the best of it). If the child learns little compared to his peers, low ability gets the blame. If actually measured intelligence (IQ) is high while performance remains average-to-poor, a *discrepancy* exists and the child is pronounced *learning disabled* and hence is a candidate for *special education*. As seen in these examples, the education system has devised a conceptual schema which places the responsibility for learning neatly on the shoulders of its pupils without placing complementary accountability on educators.

With this background, you can now tackle the task of setting a general standard for your own child's education. While this standard won't initially identify criteria of quality for each of the educational outcomes you selected in Chapter 4, it will serve as a first step in this direction.

Your initial task is to decide which combination of values among the variables—ability, expectation, achievement—best describes your child's present situation. As you begin, get input from your child and her teacher. Ask each what she perceives to be your child's ability, level of achievement, and what expectations each holds for future learning. Ask for realistic and honest input and probe for those factors that led each to her perceptions. Then in three columns on a sheet of paper headed by the three variables, write down whether each variable was rated as low, average, or high. Also record those factors that contributed to the perceptions of each variable. Next add your own estimates of these values. You will want to bring together all indicators you have of your child's present learning ability, honestly consider what expectations you have for your child's learning, and provide your estimate of her actual accomplishments. Your first step might look like this:

Figure 2

	ability	expectation	achievement
	Present Conditions		
teacher	(high to average to low)		
reasons:			
child			
reasons:			
parent			
reasons:			

Second, compare the high-average-low estimates for each of the variables as provided by your three sources. Are there discrepancies between the perceptions of teacher and child? Between child and parent? What messages are probably being given to your child with regard to these three variables by the school, by you, by your child herself?

The third step is the most difficult. Carefully reread pages 54-55 regarding the two contradictory perspectives on standards and the information on ability and expectations on pages 55-58. You may also want to revisit the list of outcomes you identified in Chapter 4 as your goals for your child's education. Then ask yourself what standard of quality is good enough for your child, and what standard of quality will be good enough for her throughout her lifetime. Asked in another way, are you willing to have your child strive to be average? It may be helpful to remember that a common synonym for *average* is *mediocre*. Is there really any standard besides excellence that makes sense for your child? For any child?

The exercise you are now completing is closely analogous to the ongoing national debate among educators about standards alluded to earlier in this chapter. The "rising tide of mediocrity" referred to in the now ten year old report *Our Nation at Risk* has led to a demand from the public for higher quality education in America, for a school system that does not strive for fifty percent of its students to be average while watching twenty-five percent drop out, and for schools that are accountable for having students meet fixed, high standards rather than the low, relative standards still in place in most public schools. Mediocrity in education poses risks, argue many political and educational leaders, to the American economic system and to our democratic way of life. Quality is indeed Job 1.

Now, if you really want to make the model of variables you've studied and the standard you've now set meaningful, you'll consult your child. Discuss the variables with him. Then ask your child if he can state the academic standard he has set for himself and how he defines the achievement of this standard. Together, write down his standard and compare it with yours. You'll become better informed through this process, and will help your child become more conscious of academic standards, yours and his. Finally, you can suggest that the two of you think about how his teacher's input figured into the factors that added up to the values you initially gave the three variables.

The teacher should, of course, be accountable too. Her recognition, for example, that perceptions of ability are often skewed could help her adjust the value of the *ability* variable she may have *fixed* for your child and could help her recognize that adjustments in your child's classroom environment might be beneficial to him. Then if she's able to adjust the value of the *ability* variable, perhaps she can simultaneously raise her expectations and set higher standards. In the outcome, your child wins.

As an interactive parent, you have every right to expect learning success for your child. You see that your child attends school regularly, is fed properly and gets needed rest, and that he has help at home with schoolwork and frequently enjoys supplemental learning activities related to his school curriculum. If your child is not meeting your standard, you can now look to both his teacher's and his own perceptions of his ability and expected performance as important clues to why. You can also, of course, consider the quality of instruction as a factor—and you will learn how to deal with problems in this area in Chapter 7. Finally, you need to examine your own level of support and interaction with both teacher and child and the messages you convey to each about your own expectations and estimates of their abilities. Your goal is to help your child get the best education possible. A high standard requires high performance—from parents as well as teachers and children.

If you encounter difficulty in setting a standard for your child because you think, or have been told, that she is either intellectually gifted or learning disabled, please read Appendix D. Setting standards for these two groups is particularly challenging, and the pitfalls of setting standards too low are equally great.

6

Monitoring
Academic Progress

In Chapter 4 you determined the goals of your child's education and identified those which you hope will be accomplished as a result of your child's schooling. You next established a general standard you want your child to meet with respect to her learning. It is a complex task, however, to ascertain whether or not this standard is being met. As an interactive parent you need to secure information about your child's academic progress, accurately interpret this information, and use it to help your child gain the most from her school experience. As an introduction to these tasks, let's look at four categories of information most schools provide: general communication, standardized achievement test scores, criterion-referenced test scores, and newer means of assessing curriculum mastery.

General School Communication

Commonly, schools report student progress to parents through three means: grade promotion or retention, parent-teacher conferences, and report cards. Unfortunately, each of these means of communication often conveys generalities and inaccuracies that can misinform parents. Educators don't always find it in their best interest to communicate too clearly about their students' academic progress. I've discovered, too, that some parents do not wish to know too precisely how well a child is learning. Detailed, accurate information about progress can lead to increased responsibilities for both the home and the school, as well as finger–pointing between these parties. In any case, the normal means of keeping parents informed about their children's progress are often inadequate. Let's look at each reporting means and its limitations and at ways you can make each as useful as possible.

Grade Promotion

Many parents assume that promotion to the next grade level at the end of the school year signifies that their child has mastered the curriculum of the completed grade. However, movement of your child to the next grade provides little indication of his present achievement level. Fifth grade classes usually include students who have mastered only a second or third grade reading level as well as students who read at levels more typical of students in grades seven and eight. In other words, your child's promotion to the next grade level provides you little, if any, information about her school performance or academic achievement. Thus, as an achievement marker, the best way to treat this information is to ignore it.

Grades on Report Cards

A second indicator of a child's academic progress is the quarterly report card, typically showing letter grades for each subject area. Report card grades can be misleading. Educational research has demonstrated that at the elementary school level, grades tend to represent a summation of several factors, only one of which is measured student performance on actual academic work. A student's physical appearance, teacher expectations, perceived student effort, and the mood or emotional state of the student all frequently contribute to letter-grade decisions. For example, some teachers, wanting all children to feel good about themselves, rarely give any student a grade below C. If you understand a C to represent average performance, and further translate this "average" concept to mean that your child is learning, for example, the fourth grade curriculum, you may one day be in for a big surprise. Letter grades can give you some idea of your child's academic progress, but only if you seek clarification of their meaning from the teacher. Seek details; ask to see your child's papers, projects, tests. Help the teacher understand that you are not questioning a particular grade, but rather are attempting to understand what that grade means with respect to your child's learning.

Parent-Teacher Conferences

Usually at the end of the first quarter of the school year parents are invited to visit the school for a parent-teacher conference. The purpose of this meeting, from an educator's perspective, is to briefly explain the child's educational program and to tell parents how well their child is progressing.

If you are an interactive parent, this parent-teacher conference is probably not needed. You will already have met your child's teacher, investigated the curriculum, and begun supportive activities at home. You certainly would not have waited until one-fourth of the school year had passed before reviewing your child's academic progress. You will probably not want to wait in line for a fifteen minute conference with an exhausted teacher who may have delivered a planned presentation to several parents before seeing you. Instead, you may wish to advise your child's teacher by note or phone that you realize how busy he will be on the day set aside for parent conferences, that you appreciate having had earlier opportunities to confer with him, and that you will be in touch when you feel that another conference is appropriate. Do indicate, however, that you will be glad to keep the appointment if the teacher considers it necessary.

If you are not yet an interactive parent and receive an invitation to a quarterly parent-teacher conference, I suggest that you not go. As mentioned above, this day is often a difficult one for the teacher. First quarter grades have just been completed and the teacher is likely to be tired. She usually has a planned routine (she reviews the report card, shows some student work, makes general statements, and so on) that may not address your concerns. The allotted fifteen or twenty minutes is insufficient time to get acquainted, let alone discuss any specifics of your child's academic progress. This parent-teacher conference will seldom provide you with the specific information you want and need, nor should it substitute for a get-acquainted meeting. I recommend that you call and advise the school secretary that it is not possible for you to come to school during the week of parent-teacher conferences, but that you are interested in having a meeting with your child's teacher after school a week or so later. Your conference time will probably have just doubled, the teacher will likely be more relaxed when he meets with you, and you will have the opportunity to pursue in greater depth some of the specific concerns you have about your child's school experience.

Standardized Achievement Test Scores

Some parents want to know how their child's performance in different subject areas compares to the performance of other children. To draw such comparisons, most schools annually administer standardized, norm-referenced tests. These tests are prepared by national testing services and are given under prescribed conditions in all schools that use them—hence they are referred to as *standardized*. Results are compared to a representative sample of a particular group of students, for example, all public school fifth graders in the U.S. These tests can serve numerous functions for school personnel besides individual student score comparisons, such as the evaluation of a particular education program within a school. Standardized achievement test results don't easily lend themselves to creative *mis*-communication. However, they can be easily misunderstood, by teachers as well as parents.

As an interactive parent you should each year review and retain a copy of your child's standardized achievement test scores. To do so, first find out from school officials which standardized test is used in your child's school, when it is given, when the results are returned to the school, and how the information is distributed to parents. Students are typically tested in the spring, and test results are sometimes not available until near the end of the school year or even after school has been dismissed for the summer. In the latter case test results are often distributed in September. Some districts do fall testing, with results usually available in December.

Second, secure a copy of all past test results that are available for your child, along with a copy of any written information that is provided for parents concerning test interpretation. You may have received copies of these test results before, or may have had them shown to you during parent-teacher conferences.

Third, study Appendix B at the back of this book, a guide to standardized test interpretation. It covers standard errors of measurement, percentile scores, grade equivalents, and other information necessary for a good understanding of standardized test results. Do not rely solely on your child's teacher to be able to correctly or fully interpret the test results to you. Some teachers can, and some clearly cannot.

Once you believe you understand a given set of test results, make an appointment with your child's teacher to see if the two of you share the same understanding. Let the teacher present his interpretations first. If you find that the two of you do not agree, discuss the issues of disagreement, and then follow-up by consulting a third party, perhaps the school counselor, the principal, another teacher, or a school psychologist. You should end up with a clear idea of how your child is doing in each subject area in comparison to students at his same grade level in your school or district, your state, and throughout the nation.

Standardized achievement test scores can provide reliable information about your child's progress, particularly when you look for trends from year to year. However, they do not provide the full picture of your child's learning, and some years may even be inaccurate—if, for example, your child was feeling sick on test day or the test was improperly administered or if your child becomes anxious in testing situations. In any case, you should begin a file of all major test results so you can track ongoing strengths and weaknesses in your child's progress as she moves through the grades.

Many parents, and educators as well, have reservations about the use of standardized achievement tests in our schools. Critics cite such factors as the tests' lack of correlation with the curriculum of a particular school, their cultural bias, their detrimental effect on student creativity, their establishment of self-fulfilling expectation levels, the stress taking them causes, etc. A new concern was raised by a 1987, fifty-state study reported in *Education Week,* which demonstrated that most states using the major standardized achievement tests were "well above the national average" in all elementary grades and subjects. The study in fact found that ninety percent of school districts and seventy percent of students who were tested scored above the average—results previously thought possible only in Lake Wobegon! Wrote the reporter, "The main purpose of the tests is looking good." So even the seemingly concrete information contained in standardized achievement test results is now being doubted.

Despite questions about them, standardized achievement tests are likely to remain in use in public schools for years to come. I wish neither to overemphasize their importance nor detail their limitations. They are simply another part of the public school environment which an interactive parent should understand and respond to appropriately.

Criterion-Referenced Tests

Many public schools lack a clear definition of just what it is that they want students to know and be able to do. Without such a definition it is impossible to state what constitutes an acceptable level of performance. When outcomes are defined, however, both parents and educators can compare children's performance against fixed and understood criteria. The type of test that results in this kind of information is called a *criterion-referenced* test, which matches your child's knowledge against a specific criterion—for example, how many basic multiplication facts the child can correctly state in a two minute period. The results show you the specific skills that your child has or has not mastered.

Teachers regularly use criterion-referenced tests as a means of determining what their students are learning. These tests may accompany textbooks and be designed by their publishers or may be teacher made. Some schools use these tests on an annual and more formal basis, often within a specific instructional program such as reading. Criterion-referenced test information may not be passed on to parents, but you can ask your child's teacher to send home or keep in a file for you any criterion-referenced tests your child takes. Seek an explanation of any test information you do not understand.

Monitoring Curriculum Mastery

Teachers regularly assess how well your child is learning the curriculum by a myriad of means—informal questioning, group and one-on-one discussion of classwork and homework, quizzes, tests, and so on.

As an important means of monitoring your child's academic progress, you should regularly review the written records of these assessments. For example, you can ask your child to bring home all written assignments. If your child is too young to manage this, arrange to have the teacher save papers for you until Friday when you (or your designee) can pick them up. You may also need to make an occasional visit to the classroom to review any workbook assignments or file of other completed work. If your child is developing a portfolio of his work at school, now and then ask him to escort you to his classroom to share his work with you. He will love doing so, and you'll learn a lot about what he knows and can do, and usually the teacher will be on hand for impromptu discussions.

Review your child's papers and tests regularly. Note scores and grades and, more importantly, keep an ongoing record of your child's successes and of the types of problems, questions, or tasks that are difficult for your child so you can track trends and provide at-home follow-up. Then when providing such follow-up, remember to emphasize that learning is the goal, not securing certain scores or grades. Over time, attempt to routinize your monitoring efforts. For example, if a social studies test is given every Friday, establish a time each weekend when you discuss test content.

As you review and discuss, check for depth and breadth of understanding and remain on the lookout for follow-up opportunities. For example, after reviewing a given assignment or test, pose some of your own problems and questions closely related to the material covered. Do not expect your child of ten to have an adult's depth of knowledge of biology or political science, but try to determine whether or not she *understands* the material she's learning. Then provide opportunities for her to practice her new skills and to apply them to new situations. If, for example, math papers indicate that your child is learning about money, you may elect to increase her involvement in family budgeting and shopping. If measurement is being taught at school, you may involve your child in cooking projects or in woodworking activities. Such home-teaching activities will help you keep track of how your child's knowledge is growing, enable you to continually reinforce her learning, allow you to share the pleasure of learning, and impart to your child some of your own ideas and values. Your child will come to realize that you are concerned with her learning, that you are willing to help, and that learning is exciting and fun to share.

If your child's progress slows down in a particular academic area, you will be quickly alerted through your routine review of her work and during your home-learning activities. When you think problems may be developing, arrange to see her teacher soon. Find out what the teacher is doing to help; find out what you can do to help.

Finally, you will want to maintain a file of your child's work. Occasionally take something from the back of the file and review it with your child to see how well the skills and concepts are being retained and to help your child develop a sense of her own progress. She'll begin to realize that learning is a continuum, a process of continuously expanding one's own body of knowledge.

Some of what I am advocating above is now being described in education literature as *alternative assessment, authentic assessment* or *performance-based assessment*. While these terms are not always used synonymously, they generally refer to the measurement of student learning by asking the child to perform a real-life task that requires the application of knowledge and skills which he has been learning. Students are thus required to actively generate responses rather than passively choose from among a set of teacher-prepared answers. Responding to a series of multiple-choice questions about writing is a different measure of learning than producing a letter to the editor of a local newspaper. Determining the number of gallons of paint required to paint a classroom is a different assessment task than completing fifteen area problems at the back of a chapter in a math text. Until schools widely adopt authentic assessment as an important tool for measuring how well students are learning, you will need to fill the gap. Your own ongoing assessment of your child's learning will provide one of the best opportunities for you to positively impact your child's education.

Monitoring curriculum mastery will require considerable interest, commitment, and effort on your part. You will want to tailor your effort to your own time and energy and share the task with other adults in your child's life. Often older siblings can help too. All will benefit.

7

Solving Problems

It's a rare child who doesn't have some problems at school over the years, most of which she can deal with herself. Now and then, however, a problem of a more serious nature develops which must be dealt with by adults. Those adults usually are school staff, not necessarily because school staff have exclusive rights to problem solving, but because the majority of parents are those silent, angry, or supportive parents that I described in Chapter 1 who tend to let the "experts" handle problems. Interactive parents, however, keep an eye out for problems that need solving and take action to investigate and solve them—oftentimes in conjunction with school staff.

Using the following problem-solving process as your guide, you can approach problems that arise in your child's educational life rationally and confidently, knowing that the steps you take will almost always produce positive results.

Recognizing A Problem

Throughout any one school year, there may be frequent occasions when you are less than pleased with an event or situation in your child's school life. Perhaps your child is involved in a tussle on the playground, gets a low grade on an assignment in part due to unclear written directions, or encounters a substitute teacher who lets classroom chaos reign for two days. These are one-time events in an imperfect system, events that, for the most part, you'll just accept. To do otherwise would be unnecessarily frustrating and counterproductive. If you feel you need to respond to such events, do so calmly, in a cooperative mode, and then move on. You may want to turn such events into learning situations for your child by discussing them with him, brainstorming ways of coping, considering the likelihood of their reoccurrence, and so on. You may find ways to offer input or assistance to school staff and, thus, turn a concern into a positive-relations building opportunity. If it appears that a given incident is or might become part of a recurring pattern, make note of it—time, date, place, incident—for later reference. For example, if your child repeatedly has trouble with older students during noon recess, an accurate log of the occurrences could help you investigate the matter later on.

When such a persistent condition negatively impacts your child's well-being or her learning, you know you have a true problem. In some instances the condition may seem clear—an incompetent teacher, a bully on the playground, or your child's consistently inappropriate behavior. In other instances the problem may be less definable and you see only symptoms. A child's poor grades or aversion to school, for example, are warning signs of deeper problems, problems that may have multiple causes, that may be solved in alternative ways, and that must be approached with care and determination.

Problem-Solving Techniques

Problem-solving techniques comprise a continuum ranging from prevention to negotiation to confrontation.

At one end, **prevention** techniques forestall the development of a problem. In Chapter 3 we looked at a preventative measure of great importance—your selection each year of your child's teacher. When we're talking of something as pervasive in your child's life as school, the value of an ounce of prevention is quite apparent.

Sometimes, at some point, problem prevention falters, leading you to **negotiation**. If, for example, your teacher selection efforts are stalled by official policy, negotiation with the principal becomes necessary. Negotiation involves a series of exchanges through which each side comes to better understand the other's perspectives and needs.

An unwillingness to compromise and the use of power can affect the process. If power is wielded, **confrontation** results. Confrontation tends to occur when one party flaunts power, when negotiations are approached from a win-lose perspective rather than win-win, when emotions block compromise, or when either side simply can't meet the needs of the other.

Your success as an interactive parent is linked to the extent to which you can remain in the prevention and negotiation stages. Here those all-important positive relations can be maintained. With confrontation, on the other hand, you'll likely arouse defensiveness among school staff, for confrontation is typically perceived by them as an attack, against which they circle the wagons, leaving you on the outside. Also, when confrontation occurs, even if you win your case, your child may lose. School staff, I'm sorry to say, can seek revenge for real or imagined defeats by displacing hostility on another available party—your child. As you can see, confrontation is best avoided whenever possible and entered into only with a clear understanding of possible consequences. One way to avoid confrontation is to follow a sound problem-solving process when true problems do occur.

Problem Solving: A Seven-Step Approach

When a problem develops that negatively affects your child's learning, you need to pursue a carefully considered plan of intervention. In some instances the problem will have been identified by you or your child, in others by school staff. While you and the staff may view the import and urgency of any problem quite differently, by following this step-by-step process, you can usually arrive at a mutually satisfying solution.

Step One: Begin to Define the Problem

As mentioned above, problems are not always readily defined. Sometimes mere uneasiness sparked by minor events develops into the recognition of a problem—a child who balks at going to school, complaints about a classmate that become too common, or hints that a teacher is belittling your child in class. At other times the nature of a problem will be immediately clear.

Always attempt to carefully define the problem. List the symptoms in precise terms. For example, if your child is "doing poorly," is he (a) not as able a reader as his friends; (b) earning low daily grades; (c) unable to demonstrate that he understands what he's studying; or (d) unable to apply math skills beyond the workbook page? In other words, specify what "doing poorly" means. Likewise, if his teacher has advised you of a problem, ask her to delineate the symptoms, to present the evidence, to define the problem precisely, in writing if possible. Ask, for example, what specific behaviors your "unruly" child exhibits, and with whom, where, and when they occur.

Step Two: Gather Information

Attempts to define the problem will often necessitate information gathering, which may involve looking through portfolios of student work, conferencing with staff, observing your child at school, discussing the problem with your child; consulting specialists, such as a school psychologist; and reviewing past data, such as achievement test scores from past years.

Information-gathering interactions need to be well planned and carefully implemented. The following three recommendations will help you in this effort.

1. Determine what specific question or questions you are attempting to answer. Refine general questions into more specific ones. For example, "How is Marty doing in school?" might best be thought of as "How does Marty's academic achievement compare with that of her peers?" or "What is Marty's present reading level?"

2. Decide who can best provide the desired information. For example, if I wished to learn how well my child was interacting with other children, I would ask not only her regular classroom teacher but also staff members who supervise the school playground.

3. You may wish to prepare a list of questions before beginning information-gathering interactions, and to actually refer to your list while meeting with school personnel. Such use can give structure to a discussion and can ensure that you do not forget an important question.

4. Always be friendly, but recognize that it is your right as a parent—and responsibility—to know all you can about your child's school experience.

Refer again to the suggestions in Chapter 2 for ways to keep your information-gathering activities positive.

Step Three: Redefine the Problem

Regardless of what you originally thought the problem was, or were told that it was, step two is likely to cause you to redefine the problem. You may have discovered that your concerns are unfounded and that a problem doesn't really exist. On the other hand, you may learn that its magnitude is greater than you thought.

As you try to define and redefine the problem, keep in mind that if it was your child's teacher or principal who brought up the problem, chances are he believes he knows what that problem is. However, while school staff have observed your child in school and have considerable experience at defining school problems, they are not privy to all of the information you possess, such as possible tensions at home, your child's educational and social history, and your child's perception of the situation. Also, school staff may view the problem from the perspective of its negative impact on the school rather than on your child. In fact, in some instances the problem can be more accurately described as their problem with your child. But regardless of who initiates the problem-solving process, you'd be wise to follow all seven steps.

Step Four: Establish an Acceptable Outcome

Once you have defined the problem, you need to identify the outcome you seek, at which you will focus your problem-solving intervention. An outcome is acceptable if it enables your child to regain his well-being and be a successful learner, however you define success. The outcome should be observable—so that you will *know* whether or not it has been achieved. Thus an outcome that calls for your child to "do better in school" is too vague, as compared to one that calls for your child to increase particular reading skills during the school year. The outcome should provide a long-lasting solution, if possible, so that the problem will not return, and should be achievable within the reality of the school situation.

Step Five: Generate Alternative Routes

As the dimensions of a problem become clearer, you may quickly identify a single means of solving it. Certainly there are situations for which the solution is immediately clear; however, problems are often more complex. You'll be wise, in either case, to avoid becoming immediately committed to one course of action because you may be overlooking better alternatives for achieving the desired outcome. Instead, brainstorm all possible alternatives, even those that seem ludicrous or unmanageable at first glance. Then consider the response of school staff to your alternatives—particularly those alternatives which might be difficult for them to implement.

Ask your child's teacher, other school staff, and your child for ideas too. Explain the problem concisely from your perspective. State what you believe is an appropriate outcome—what it is you hope to achieve. Then ask for suggestions about how to accomplish this outcome. You'll probably want to avoid sharing your own ideas at this point. You are trying to generate as many suggestions from others as possible. Your statement of possible solutions could be interpreted as proposals, which would likely cause educators to shift to an evaluative mode rather than freely brainstorming different possibilities.

Consider this example: Imagine that you have a child who cries and gets angry every morning before leaving for school. These symptoms suggest to you that he doesn't like school, and you suspect that a poor teacher is the reason.

You initially decide that the solution is to have him placed in another classroom. By following the above steps, however, you learn that your child dislikes going to school because his teacher frequently disciplines him for breaking class rules. Now it is clear that you'll need to gather more information: Are the rules reasonable? Are other children able to follow them? Why might your child have trouble following them? Do the teacher's disciplinary methods allow your child's self-esteem to remain intact? Do they reinforce the bad behavior? Do you need to observe your child and his teacher in action? Once you've gathered all the information you can, you'll return to the task of identifying the outcome you want and generating solutions. You'll be back to the question, "What specifically can I, the teacher, and my child do to improve the situation?"

Then with a number of alternatives in hand, evaluated too for their consequences, you'll be ready to take the next step, developing and committing to a plan.

Step Six: Develop an Action Plan

Alternatives in hand, narrow the list to those two or three which you believe have the highest probability of success. Then arrange a meeting with those school staff you'll need to involve in carrying out your plan. Review the problem with them and state the desired outcome. Try to elicit their agreement to this same result. Note that you've consulted with all parties involved and have gathered various ideas on possible solutions. Then propose your alternatives. State that you believe now is the time to act and ask the staff which alternative they believe would lead to the desired outcome.

Be forewarned! You may be met with an initial response of uncertain silence. Teachers and principals are not accustomed to dealing with interactive, problem-solving parents. School personnel may feel uneasy about having you assume such an active role and may need time to get accustomed to you. Friendly smiles and genuine interest in their opinions and positions will help alleviate their apprehension. Recognize that one or more of your proposed alternatives may be difficult for the staff to implement. Listen well and be flexible. You may even be presented with more alternatives. Again, listen, consider all routes to the outcome, but do remain committed to the outcome itself.

You may find yourself negotiating. To negotiate effectively, you need to identify what the other party or parties need and want. They may, for example,

- want to see your child succeed in school;

- need your assistance with solving the problem;

- want a solution that doesn't infringe upon other children or on class routines;

- want a solution that is easy to implement;

- want a solution that will mollify you;

- need to uphold district policies;

- want to uphold traditional practices;

- want to contain the problem at the lowest possible level.

Knowing their wants and needs will enable you to spot opportunities to let them win while you win too. Such information will also help you determine which obstacles you need to sensitively, skillfully find ways to circumvent. Listen carefully for clues to their greatest needs; ask clarifying questions to help you further identify what these needs are. Let them know some of your own interests as well, such as getting the problem solved in the most effective manner possible and avoiding any escalation of the matter beyond those staff with whom you are now engaged.

At some point your conference will either end in agreement, by settling on one alternative, or with a stalemate. In the latter case, retreat (with a smile) to strategize. If, on the other hand, a course of action is agreed upon, the conference should quickly turn to implementation planning. Together outline your common understanding of an action plan. Be sure everyone understands—

why the plan is being implemented (the identified problem and the outcome you want to achieve);

who will play a role in the plan (teacher, parent, principal, child, other school staff);

what specific actions each individual will take;

when these actions will occur;

where they will occur.

Visibly record the agreed-upon elements of the plan and then at the end of the conference read it aloud in review to make certain that all agree to the plan and to their individual responsibilities. Jot down what you all consider visible evidence that the outcome has been reached. Then forthrightly state that you will be watching closely for that evidence. Be sure, too, that you've all considered the longterm—that you've agreed, not upon a stop-gap solution, but a permanent one. If you haven't, take time now to identify ways of maintaining the desired outcome once it has been achieved.

Step Seven: Implement and Evaluate

You must, of course, carry out any part of the plan that you agreed specifically to accomplish, and you'll need to monitor with a reasonable measure of patience the activities of the involved others. A well-intentioned teacher or principal can easily fall behind schedule due to unpredictable circumstances. When this happens, deliver gentle, helpful reminders—which may even be appreciated. Keep a record of these contacts, however. If it becomes necessary to be more insistent, you can refer to your earlier and more positive attempts to ensure action.

Your evaluation of the process depends upon the outcome—namely, whether or not it has been reached at the child level. Refer back to your statement of the desired outcome. Can you or your child's teacher now cite concrete evidence of its achievement? In the example given above, the parent would need to know whether or not his child is now following the classroom rules or the teacher has tried a more successful disciplinary method, and whether the morning symptoms are now gone.

If your problem-solving plan works, you'll have an excellent opportunity to thank the individuals whose efforts led to success. Don't forget to express your appreciation to their supervisors as well. A note to a superintendent, for instance, stating how much you appreciated your principal's assistance in solving the problem, can help reaffirm the positive relations you may have bruised a bit during the negotiating process. You could give a copy of the note to the principal, too, as a way of directly reinforcing her effort.

If the agreed upon plan has not worked within the expected period of time, you must determine whether the failure was due to nonimplementation of plan activities, or whether the plan itself was faulty. In the latter case, you'll need to revisit the problem and develop a new plan. If the plan was simply not implemented, try not to become an angry parent. Instead, refine your understanding of the situation and of the needs of those with whom you are dealing and try again. Your persistence will likely stimulate action as school staff realize you are not going to give up. However, if persistence doesn't reap results, you'll then need to consider using the *chain-of-command.*

The Chain-of-Command

Like most bureaucracies, the public school system is hierarchical, and in a hierarchical system you rarely need to accept "no" for an answer because you can always appeal to the next higher level. The interactive parent needs to understand a public school's chain-of-command and when and how to use it.

At the bottom of the ladder is the classroom teacher. Teachers work under the supervision of an administrator, the principal. In some schools there may also be an assistant principal, though you will typically not need to consider him as part of the chain unless your problem falls within the perimeters of his role in the school.

The principal's supervisor will in most instances be the school district's superintendent, though in large school districts perhaps an assistant superintendent. A superintendent works under the auspices of the governing body of the school district, the school board or board of trustees, which sets district policies and approves the curriculum, the annual budget, and such. The board is regulated by state statutes and federal law and is responsive to the public.

If problem-solving negotiations have proven unsuccessful, you may need to either take negotiations to a level higher in the chain or move to the far end of the continuum, to confrontation, starting at the bottom of the hierarchy. In either case, revisit your problem-solving steps and replan as needed. Then make your new attempt. If once again negotiations don't work, or confrontation doesn't succeed at the lowest level, you'll need to consider pursuing the issue at the next higher level in the chain-of-command.

You'll also use the chain-of-command when the solution to a problem requires decisions or actions that cannot be accomplished at the level at which you are interacting. A teacher cannot, for example, transfer a child to another classroom, and a principal cannot unilaterally change school district policy.

Keep in mind the following factors with respect to the chain-of-command:

1. You will always be expected to address your problem first to the lowest level in the hierarchy that has the ability or authority to deal with it. For example, a complaint to a principal about a teacher will probably lead to the question of whether or not you have talked with the teacher. If a principal has the authority to deal with a problem you are presenting to the school board, you will be directed to address your concerns to the principal. A sound approach is always to begin with the teacher, even when you don't think he has the authority to deal with the problem. You may pick up an ally, and you won't later have to deal with the frustration of being remanded to a lower court. As usual, there are exceptions to this general advice. For example, you would want to go directly to the principal if you have reason to believe that a teacher is being abusive to children.

2. If you are unable to resolve a problem at a given level and decide to go to a higher level in the chain, tell the person with whom you are presently working. This announcement may bring about a sudden willingness to negotiate. It also avoids placing the individual in a position of surprise or embarrassment. Remember, too, that considerable care should be taken not to step on those who occupy the various rungs of the hierarchy as you appeal to the next level because you need friends and supporters at all positions on the ladder. You are trying to solve a problem but are not in pursuit of a costly victory.

3. Document your efforts at all levels. You may later need to refer to dates, agreements, actions, the content of conversations, data you've gathered, and so on.

4. Remain open to new ideas that might resolve the issue and to new people who may offer input.

Hopefully, you won't need to take a problem up the chain-of-command. Hopefully, you'll be able to operate almost all of the time on the prevention end of the prevention-negotiation-confrontation problem-solving continuum and to develop enduring positive relationships with school staff in the process.

However ...what if your best efforts just don't work, or what if the problems you identify in your child's school that directly impact her education are simply too great for you to resolve? The final chapter of this book addresses these two questions by looking at other options.

8

Considering Alternatives

If this book has been sufficiently convincing, you have decided to be an interactive parent—to be the active overseer of your child's education. If this is the case, I urge you to continually refer to previous chapters and the appendices in this book as you carry on your interactions with school staff throughout your child's schooling years.

I recognize, however, that some parents may wish to consider alternatives that go beyond their children's present schooling situation. Perhaps frustration, lack of control, and roadblocks will lead you to seek real independence. Perhaps your best attempts at interactive parenting prove unsuccessful, or perhaps an excellent teacher is simply not available at your child's grade level in a given school year. Then it's time to explore alternatives within the public school system as well as outside of it. Let's consider three possibilities.

Alternatives Within Public Education

Classrooms vary greatly; schools vary greatly. Each school is a unique learning environment, with its own atmosphere, standards, levels of expectation, instructional strategies, degree of caring, pride, discipline, etc. If you are dissatisfied with your child's education program at a given school and have exhausted possibilities for improvement within that school setting, consider transferring your child to another public school. Of course, if you live in a small community with a single elementary and high school, this won't be possible. If you live in a multi-school district, however, use the recommendations in this book for information gathering and establishing positive relationships as you explore another school. You may need your problem-solving skills to actually bring about the transfer. Then use the steps outlined for selecting a teacher as you enroll your child in his new school. Here are a few more hints:

1. As you examine other schools, be thorough. Don't attempt the transfer process until you are confident that the new school can better meet your child's needs.

2. Expect to be told initially that all children who live within prescribed geographic boundaries must attend a particular school. Consider this to be a bureaucratic response and use your interactive skills to pursue the matter further. I do not suggest that this will be an easy task. School officials frequently wish to avoid granting to parents the opportunity to select a school for their child because it could lead to a recognition by parents of disparities in the quality of schools and increasing numbers of transfer requests.

3. Consult with parents of students in the school you are considering. Ask about the degree to which they are encouraged by the school to be partners in the education process. Often a school's quality varies according to the number of interactive parents it serves. A school superintendent must pay greater attention to neighborhoods with active, participatory parents, school staffs will tend to be better due to both district and self-selection processes, and teachers' academic expectations will typically be higher.

4. In some instances you may wish to consider actually moving your residence across school district or attendance area boundary lines so that your child will be able (and required) to attend a different school.

5. It is also sometimes possible to keep your current residence, but send your child to a school in

another school district. You will need to provide transportation and to pay out-of-district tuition. Both of these expenses are likely to be less than the cost of private schooling, however.

6. Always remember that you may find an outstanding teacher in a school reputed to be a poor one.

7. Finally, some school districts have established what are referred to as alternative schools—designed for a particular type of student, focused on particular subject areas or student talents such as the sciences or performing arts, or embracing a unique educational philosophy. In some locations these schools are referred to as magnet schools, attracting to them students from a wider area than their typical school neighborhood. A major purpose of such schools is to formalize options for parents and hence avoid parental dissatisfaction while enhancing student opportunities for success. Generally, education journals report positive parent satisfaction with, and student academic success in, these public alternative schools. Be forewarned, however, that waiting lists and student entrance requirements may pose enrollment problems.

8. Advocates of "school choice" have placed the issue of parents selecting which school their children will attend firmly on state and national political agendas. Some school districts now allow parents to choose among all schools in the district, and some state legislatures are expanding this freedom of choice to any public school within any district in a given state. Those who favor even greater competition to public education wish to extend this parent option to private schools as well. The trend is thus in the direction of increased parental options for choosing an education program considered best for your children, alternatives which an interactive parent will be well prepared to consider.

Private Schooling

In some communities the monopoly of public education is challenged by one or more private schools. Private education takes many forms, from parochial schools to neighborhood classrooms established by an involved parents' association. Private schools often have a unique character or tradition—a social climate based upon a common set of values. They thus bring together a set of parents that share similar moral, cultural, or intellectual preferences.

If one or more private schools exist in your community, you have an obvious alternative to public education. As you consider this option, think about these issues:

1. It is unwise to make generalizations about private schools. Some are excellent, some average, some poor. Individual teacher quality will vary, as it does in public schools. Tight budgets can limit the purchase of up-to-date instructional materials, lab equipment, computers. Some political, social, and/or scientific viewpoints may not be represented or over-represented in the curriculum. While it may be easier to remove poor teachers from private schools, in some instances it is harder to attract and keep good teachers due to lower salaries and sometimes the lack of fringe benefits.

2. Quality education can be expensive. If a private school is operated for profit, you can expect to pay accordingly for the services. If the school is subsidized, the funding organization may be paying for the opportunity to have access to your child. In other words, its values may be a regular feature of both the overt and hidden curriculums. If these values are shared by you, and if you are confident that you want your child to learn them, subsidized private education may provide a good opportunity for your child. If such is not the case, a bargain private education may prove to be expensive indeed.

3. Some private schools are "creativity" schools—teaching, for instance, to musical, theatrical, or

literary talents. You'll need to identify any specialty curriculum areas emphasized by the private schools you consider and ask yourself (and your child) if these emphases are suitable for your child. If you find a private school that does focus on the special talents and interests of your child, she is likely to flourish there.

4. Private schools must provide customer satisfaction. They tailor their programs to the needs of a particular clientele and must satisfy parents to remain in business. Interactive parenting should therefore be easier in such a setting.

In summary, I urge you to examine carefully any private school you consider rather than assume that it will provide your child a better education. Again, you will want to visit the school, talk with administrators, observe teachers, talk with the children who attend and with their parents, and look at the curriculum. Only then can you decide if a private school is the best alternative.

The number of private elementary and secondary schools in the United States is growing rapidly, so apparently many parents are electing this educational alternative for their children. A study of the occupations of parents who send their children to private schools in an eastern state revealed that private schooling was no longer the almost exclusive bastion of parents in the legal and medical professions. Interestingly, in fact, the single largest occupational group of the parents of children in these private schools was public school administrators!

Home Schooling

Home schooling refers to a situation in which parents teach their child in the home in lieu of having the child attend public or private school. Home schooling is sometimes a necessity with children who live far away from a public school and cannot attend due to transportation difficulties. Most present-day home-school parents, however, elect to home school because they believe they will do a better job of educating their children than will the public schools.

The answers to the following five questions provide a brief introduction to the home-schooling alternative:

Is home schooling legal?

Every state has some form of compulsory school attendance law, usually stated in terms of an age range within which a child must attend school, and penalties may be meted out to parents who allow truancy. These laws are being increasingly challenged in the courts, however. Due to growing pressure from swelling numbers of home schoolers, several states have recently amended their compulsory school attendance laws or have adopted statutes which specifically address home schooling.

The late author and educator John Holt noted emerging case law in a chapter of his 1981 book titled *Teach Your Own*, from which the following summary of the legality issue is derived.

The Law Summed Up

1. Parents have a right to educate their children in whatever way they believe best; the state cannot impose on all parents any kind of educational monopoly, of schools, methods, or whatever. ...

2. The state may not deprive parents of the right to home school for arbitrary reasons, but only for serious educational ones, which it must make known to parents, with all the forms of due process. ...

3. A state that would deny parents these rights by saying that their home-education plan is inadequate has a burden of proof to show beyond reasonable doubt that this is so. Parents are assumed to be competent to teach their children until proved otherwise. This Assumption of Competence is kin to and part of the general Assumption of Innocence (of the accused) which holds in all criminal proceedings. ...

4. In order to prove that the parents' education plans are inadequate, the state must show that its own

requirements, regulations, etc., are educationally necessary and do in fact produce, in its own schools, better results than the parents get or are likely to get. ...

You will find that some school districts are much more familiar with the compulsory school laws of their state than they are with the broader interpretation of such laws by the courts. Nevertheless, advising them of this information should cause their reconsideration of possible legal posturing should you want to home school your children. Usually, certain requirements must be met by home-schooling parents, such as the presentation to the local school district of a planned curriculum. The best way to begin exploring these matters is to contact one of the many home-school organizations existing in our country today.

What are the special skills or characteristics of parents who home-school their children?

The notion that one must be a certified or formally trained teacher in order to successfully teach is increasingly becoming recognized as untrue. But some characteristics are important. Home-schooling parents need, for instance, to be able to organize materials, locate and use resources of all kinds, and be creative. They certainly do not need to be college graduates nor to have undergone any formal post-secondary education, nor even to be textbook savvy. Holt suggests a number of additional characteristics that define the successful home-schooling parent:

> We can sum up very quickly what people need to teach their own children. First of all, they have to *like* them, enjoy their company, their physical presence, their energy, foolishness, and passion. They have to enjoy all their talk and questions, and enjoy equally trying to answer those questions. They have to think of their children as friends, indeed very close friends, have to feel happier when they are near and miss them when they are away. They have to trust them as people, respect their fragile dignity, treat them with courtesy, take them

seriously. They have to feel in their own hearts some of the children's wonder, curiosity, and excitement about the world. And they have to have enough confidence in themselves, skepticism about experts, and willingness to be different from most people, to take on themselves the responsibility for their children's learning.

Currently several hundred thousand parents throughout the nation are home-schooling, and increasing numbers of research studies demonstrate that most of their children are thriving academically.

How much time will home schooling take each day?

Children attend public school approximately six hours per day. Carefully conducted research has shown, however, that the amount of actual instructional time per day in most classrooms is about four hours and twenty minutes, and each child is probably not actively engaged in learning for more than eighty-five percent of that instructional time. The net result—brought about to a great extent by a teacher's need to instruct twenty or thirty youngsters—is that during a typical public school day your child is actively engaged in the learning process no more than three hours. Home-schooling parents thus typically do not find it necessary to duplicate a regular school schedule.

Home-schooling parents report, by the way, that there are teachers available to a home-school child other than the child's parents. A retired person in the neighborhood, a community librarian, an older sibling, a scientist, a musician, a scout leader—all can offer learning experiences to a home-school child by participating in part of the child's custom-designed curriculum.

I don't wish to suggest that home schooling doesn't require a great amount of time and energy on the part of parents. It is simply important for you to understand that it does not need to involve you in a direct teaching role for six hours a day.

Are educational materials and resources available to home schoolers?

The number of resources available to home-schooling parents is great. Parents can secure special learning kits, such as in art or music, or can buy a complete home-school program that contains all lessons and materials needed for a school year. Some of these programs are affiliated with a particular school or resource center which provides various support services as well. Also, almost all of the materials available to public school teachers are available to parents through catalogs, bookstores, and school supply houses.

And don't forget computers. A new age of home instruction is emerging in the form of computer software and networks. Instruction is available in languages, all levels of mathematics, English composition, typing, the sciences, and much much more—in forms that vary from rote drill-and-practice to sophisticated interactive communications between student and computer.

How do home-schooled children learn social interaction skills?

Some parents who consider home schooling are concerned that their children will not spend sufficient time with other children. Home schoolers are quick to point out, however, that many playmates become available after school hours each day, that there are lots of clubs and organizations for kids, summer recreation programs, camps, home-schoolers' gatherings, and other people of all ages in the community. It is, in fact, part of the limited, peer-dependent social setting of the public school and the informal learning experiences engendered in that social setting that many home-schooling parents wish to avoid.

It's possible, too, to have the best of both worlds, home school and public school. For example, through effective interaction, arrangements might be made with public school officials for your home-school child to attend music, art, or physical education classes, to use the school library, or perhaps even to participate in some extracurricular activities.

Regardless of the alternative you choose—public, private, or home schooling—your talents as an interactive parent will be important to ensuring the quality of your child's education.

Epilogue

Reading, 'riting and 'rithmetic may have been public education's 3 R's during the first ninety years of the twentieth century, but the 1990's are witness to their replacement: reform, restructuring, and revolution. Today the very beliefs that prescribe much of what occurs in public schools are under scrutiny—by educators as well as by a disenchanted public. Major improvements in public education may result, but meanwhile your child is growing older and you have a choice to make.

- You can choose to be a silent parent, relegating all responsibility for your child's education to the public school "experts." Even if your child now achieves at an above-average level, do remember that public education's concept of *average* has evolved out of a system designed to mass-produce mediocrity.

- You can choose to be an angry parent, wasting time and energy fighting the system, often ignoring your child's best interests while attempting to achieve your own ends.

- You can choose to be a supportive parent, trading volunteer time, praise, cookies, and patience for the measure of friendliness and consideration that will come your way. Your child may be treated kindly in return too, but his learning isn't likely to be greatly affected.

- You can opt out of the public school system and become a private-school or home-schooling parent.

- You can elect to be an interactive parent, optimistically, methodically, persistently engaging the
  school in order to secure for your child the best
  available public school education.

You will make one of these choices. I am hoping this
book will help you become an interactive parent, for I
believe your child deserves the best bite of the apple. Don't
you think so too?

Suggested Readings

Note: The following is a starter list. Once you've become familiar with these books, look for others. These titles are available at your local bookstore, library, or through inter-library loan.

Art From Found Materials by Mary Lou Stribling (Crown, 1970).

The Backyard Scientist; Series Four by Jane Hoffman (Backyard Scientist, 1992). Also Series One, Two, and Three.

Books Kids Will Sit Still For: A Guide to Using Children's Literature for Librarians, Teachers, and Parents (Alleyside Press, 1984).

Cultural Literacy; What Every American Needs to Know by E. D. Hirsch, Jr. (Houghton Mifflin, 1987).

Developmentally Appropriate Practice in Early Childhood Programs Serving Children From Birth Through Age 8; expanded edition, edited by Sue Bredekamp (National Association for the Education of Young Children, 1986).

Families Writing by Peter Stillman (Writer's Digest Books, 1989).

Getting Together: Building Relationships As We Negotiate by Roger Fisher and Scott Brown (Penguin Books, 1989).

Getting To Yes: Negotiating Agreement Without Giving In by Roger Fisher and William Ury (Penguin Books, 1981).

Home School: Taking the First Step by Borg Hendrickson (Mountain Meadow Press, 1990).

How to Write a Low-Cost/No-Cost Curriculum for Your Home-School Child by Borg Hendrickson (Mountain Meadow Press, 1990).

The Learning Mystique: A Critical Look at Learning Disabilities by Gerald Coles (Pantheon, 1987).

Literacy Development Through Family Reading by Mina Hassman (Ashley Books, 1990).

The New Read-Aloud Handbook by Jim Trelease (Penguin Books, 1989).

The New York Times Parent's Guide to Best Books for Children by Eden Ross Lipson (Times Books, 1988).

A Parent's Guide to Books for Teens and Preteens by Arthea Reed (International Reading Association).

Parents, Schools and the Law by David Schimmel and Louis Fischer (National Committee for Citizens in Education, 1987).

Taking Books to Heart; How to Develop a Love of Reading in Your Child by Paul Copperman (Addison-Wesley, 1986).

Taming the Homework Monster by Ellen Klavan (Poseidon Press, 1992).

Your Gifted Child and You by Felice Kaufman (Council for Exceptional Children, 1983).

Appendix A

Classroom Observation Guidelines

As part of the process of selecting the best available teacher for your child, you'll want to make classroom observations. The guidelines below will help you become organized for this task and provide you with a format for recording the results. The guidelines are intended as a supplement to Chapter 3, which includes a list of effective teacher behaviors and suggestions for arranging and conducting observations.

I recommend that you focus your observations on four main elements: classroom management, quality of instruction, emotional atmosphere, and personal response.

Classroom Management

You will recall that actual learning time during the school day varies by classroom and sometimes amounts to as little as fifty percent of a child's total time in school. The objective of classroom management techniques should be the maximization of learning time—involving both teacher instructional time and student *engaged* learning time. To determine whether or not a teacher is maximizing learning time, consider these questions:

Is there evidence of procedural routines?

If three children individually interrupt a teacher working with a reading group to ask about routine procedures, you know that time is regularly wasted on such matters. If procedural rules are posted and/or if students appear to go about their activities in a nondisruptive way, procedural routines are in effect. I do not suggest here that regimental order is needed. In fact, in some classrooms, what may initially appear to be disorder could actually be a class of very involved learners. Procedural rules simply smooth the way for maximal use of both the teacher's and students' time for teaching and learning.

How much time is used making transitions from one learning activity to another?

Some teachers can miraculously move thirty eight-year-olds engaged in four learning activities into a single class in under two minutes, while others take five times as long. Thirty minutes of instruction lost each day in inefficient transitioning means your child will lose three full weeks of instruction during the school year. I suggest no standard here—obviously transition time will vary with the size and composition of the class, the nature of the learning activities, etc. You will quickly see, however, whether or not students are reengaged in learning within a reasonable length of time.

How much time is devoted to disciplinary efforts?

Some teachers are constantly attempting to "straighten out" one or more students, sometimes reinforcing the very behavior they wish to eliminate. Other teachers rarely have disciplinary problems. Disciplining a student takes time away from instruction and focuses student attention away from learning. If maintaining discipline is consuming too much time in a classroom you are observing, you will quickly become aware of this fact.

How much time does the class spend on noninstructional activities?

Some teachers appear to be interested in doing whatever keeps the children entertained, busy, or quiet, or in some other way helps the teacher get through the day. Other teachers appear driven to fill their limited time with every possible bit of instruction and to avoid interruptions and meaningless activity.

How much of the time are students actively engaged in learning?

You may be tempted while observing a classroom to concentrate on observing the teacher, but at least half the time should be spent watching children. I have observed teachers who appeared to be doing a good job of presenting a lesson—while students wrote notes to each other, read comic books, and generally ignored the teacher. Are the students actively engaged with the teacher or with independent learning exercises? How many appear to be drifting or confused or unengaged in the learning process? If your child were in this class, what would she be doing?

Quality of Instruction—During Lesson Delivery

The quality of instruction will obviously impact your child's learning. Research continues to identify the ingredients of a quality lesson, usually regardless of subject matter or grade level. I have drawn from this research four steps in a well-executed lesson. You may not see all four during a single instructional period—perhaps the complete lesson has been divided into two sessions, or maybe one part required more time than anticipated, necessitating a continuance. However, you will probably see all of these elements in the course of watching two lessons in different subject areas.

Setting the Stage

Critical to each new lesson is a dynamic introduction that ignites the interest of the learners. Look for pizzazz, enthusiasm, excitement. Next, the teacher should explain to his students the purpose of the lesson, sometimes stated in terms of what they will know or be able to do at the completion of the lesson (the lesson's outcome.) Finally, a good lesson introduction also relates the content of the lesson to the students' own backgrounds and experiences, to other parts of the curriculum, and/or to the world outside the classroom. All of this can be briefly presented orally or with a quick demonstration. The lesson's opening is critical, however, for it generates curiosity and provides students with a sense of the lesson's direction and of their own learning task.

Delivering Instruction

This part of a lesson involves presenting or helping students discover new information through a lecture, demonstration, experiment, film, reading passage, exploration activity, or any combination of these and other techniques. Direct instruction and exploratory activities should clearly lead towards the lesson's outcome. The teacher should be frequently checking student understanding and clarifying concepts through examples and demonstrations as needed.

Guided Practice

While new information is fresh in students' minds, they need an opportunity to apply the information, perhaps by relating concepts to one another, practicing skills, or in some other way incorporating the skills and information into whole, meaningful tasks. The teacher guides and facilitates to make certain students understand the material and provides direct feedback to the learners.

Independent Application

In this phase of a lesson each student uses the learned skills or information in a new context, through which he demonstrates understanding. Independent activities take various forms, such as using new vocabulary words in a creative writing exercise, completing math story problems, creating models, or planning a presentation. If the lesson was well presented, each student should be reasonably successful during independent application. This phase also includes some form of assessment by the teacher, to determine the success of the lesson and to identify those students who appeared to be doing okay during guided practice but who nevertheless now appear to need further teaching.

These four major elements of a good lesson provide you with a basic framework for your observations. As a follow-up, ask yourself: Did the lesson include these four elements? Was the instruction clear? Did most of the children in the instructional group appear to understand it? Would your child have understood it? Did students appear eager to try out their new information in the guided practice?

Was the practice truly guided, or did the teacher "take a break" while it was underway? You will quickly generate additional questions as you watch a class in action. Also, be sure to refer back to Chapter 3 for a refresher on effective teaching practices.

Quality of Instruction—When Teacher is "Facilitator"

During the guided practice stage of the above described lesson, to an extent during independent practice, and at any time students are singly or in groups working on an activity or project, the teacher, if she wants to be effective, will circulate among students facilitating their learning process. She will, in fact, already have served as facilitator by setting the stage, or arranging the props, for the activities being done around the room.

Particularly in primary education (grades K-3), facilitation vs. "teaching" has become more common, due in large part to research which shows that young children learn best when activity options are available for free choice. The teacher in this role facilitates choice and learning by designing activity stations throughout the classroom that entice student participation and that are geared towards appropriate learner outcomes. At the same time, these activity stations allow for students to work at varied ability levels, that is, each at his own level.

When you are observing a teacher who is acting as facilitator, watch for these factors in her behavior:

1. Does she circulate? Does she at some point make contact with every student?

2. Does she encourage each child's exploration? Does she encourage risk-taking? Does she convey trustworthiness so that students feel safe enough to take exploratory risks?

3. Does she stimulate diverse thinking through input, questions, and prompts?

4. Does she offer useful feedback?

When you are observing a classroom designed with activity stations, look as closely as you can, without interfering, at the activities themselves. Do the activities stimulate diverse thinking, exploration, and discovery learning? Do they seem purposeful? Can you tell what their academic objectives or intended outcomes are? If the answer to these questions is *yes*, you can fairly reliably conclude that the teacher-facilitator is skillful at designing the learning environment.

Emotional Atmosphere

Classrooms vary in emotional atmosphere. They may be tense, competitive, impersonal, warm, cooperative, chaotic, energizing, business-like, and so on. To assess the emotional atmosphere of a classroom, imagine for a period of time that you are your child, deeply involved in all that goes on in the room. What would your child feel? Consider the following:

1. Is there excitement in this room, a sense that something interesting is continuously happening, or do the hours and minutes proceed in a dull and routinized fashion?

2. Does the teacher appear to offer individualized attention and recognition to her students, or do many students appear to be lost in the group?

3. Does the teacher express high expectations for all students, along with a sense of confidence that they can succeed, or does mediocrity appear to be acceptable, or even expected?

4. Does the teacher provide warm support and encouragement to all students, or does she discourage students with belittlement and embarrassment, display mistrust, or act in other ways which downgrade students?

5. Does she seem sensitive to and respectful of individual personalities, ethnicities, problems, and needs? Does she handle problems swiftly, quietly, effectively?

6. How do the children interact with each other? Do you see mostly cooperation or competition? (Allow

for some disagreements in every classroom, particularly in the elementary grades.)

While these emotional variables are extracted from what research tells us constitutes effective teaching, you may wish to add some of your own that you believe are important and which relate specifically to your child. Remember also that children can be very sensitive to what happens to other children. For example, even if your child is not likely to be the one who gets yelled at, the yelling itself (at any child) can damage the relationship between your child and her teacher and diminish your child's pleasure in learning.

Personal Response

As an interactive parent you need to enter a close working relationship with your child's teacher—one of mutual trust, support, respect, and positive regard. Your ability to do so may in part depend upon how you personally respond to the teacher. If she appears to do an excellent job of teaching but in personal conversation makes you feel very uncomfortable and put-down, you may want to consider an alternative. Be leery, too, of selecting a teacher who is a personal friend, at least until you have observed her teaching. She may not be able to deliver a quality lesson or may not meet other criteria for which you are looking. However, good teachers are often personally effective, too, and easy to like. A shared goal—the education of your child—and your willingness to assist can provide the basis for an excellent relationship. In any case, do pay attention to your personal responses to prospective teachers.

You may still be apprehensive about actually observing a teacher and students in the classroom. You will become much more comfortable with this process after just one classroom visit.

The following summary of the above material will help you establish a format for conducting and recording your observations. You can prepare a set of note cards or other convenient form to guide you.

Classroom Management

Evidence of procedural rules
Discipline and transition time, amount and effect
Teacher instructional time, amount and use
Student engaged time, amount and purpose

Quality of Instruction During Lesson Delivery

Setting the Stage

Interest Arousal
Explanation of lesson's purpose
Prior knowledge and content relationships

Delivering Instruction

Information clearly presented
Activities directed to lesson's intended outcomes
Student understanding is monitored

Guided Practice

Guided practice provided
Individual feedback given
Activities directed to lesson outcomes

Independent Application

Application activities provided
Student assessment conducted

Quality of Instruction When Teacher is Facilitator

Stage is set to stimulate exploration, thinking, and
    discovery learning
Activities directed towards learner outcomes
Teacher circulates
Teacher questions, prompts and provides feedback

Emotional Atmosphere

Classroom excitement/interest level
Individual recognition of students
Teacher expectation level

Warmth and encouragement vs. belittlement
Sensitivity to individual differences
Tone of peer interaction among students

Personal Response

Your emotional reaction to the person who is teacher

Appendix B

Interpreting Standardized Achievement Test Results

Chapter 6 introduced you to various tests administered in public schools and suggested ways for you to use test results. Below is a brief primer on standardized achievement tests and their correct interpretation.

What is a standardized test?

A standardized test is one that is administered, scored and interpreted in a standardized or formalized manner. All students who take the test are given the same directions, the same test items, and the same amount of time to complete the test. Because it is standardized, it is possible to establish test norms consisting of the scores of many students from a wide sample of a given population (for example, all third graders in the U.S.). Using the norms, educators can make comparisons between the performance of individuals and that of the students in the norm group.

What about a test's validity?

A major concern is whether or not a particular test actually measures student achievement on a given curriculum. If students aren't taught multiplication in your child's second grade classroom, it isn't appropriate to administer a test that measures multiplication skills. In other words, there needs to be a match between the class' curriculum content and the content of the test administered to a student who has progressed through that curriculum. You may wish to ask school personnel how they determined the content validity of the test they are using. Sometimes sizeable discrepancies exist between the skills and knowledge taught and those measured by the achievement test, and this lack of congruity can bring into question the test's validity.

The validity question may also be raised if your child is a minority child, a bilingual child whose first language is not English, or a child who lives outside mainstream America. The content of achievement tests is based upon common experiences and background of mainstream American children. For example, a transportation item on the test isn't likely to include dog sleds, but may include subways, and thus baffle the Eskimo student, for whom the test's validity may be doubted.

How reliable are my child's scores on standardized tests?

Test *reliability* refers to the consistency with which your child would achieve the same test score on the identical test taken on several occasions. In Chapter 6, I pointed out that any given test score is a measurement of how your child performed on a given test at a particular time, when administered under a unique set of circumstances. It is possible that a child feels ill on test day, that the test administrator accidentally allowed three extra minutes for a section of the test, that the teacher felt tense and created tension among the test takers, that the test itself contained flaws, or any number of other possible circumstances that can produce questionable test results.

Test makers assume that a "true score" exists for your child on a given test, and that all measurements made are approximations of this true score. Thus any single score is actually an estimate representing a band within which we can be confident that a student's true score lies.

What else do I need to know to understand my child's achievement test scores?

The test scores that are of greatest interest to parents are percentile, grade equivalent, and possibly age equivalent. Other test scores, such as normal curve equivalents and stanines, are mostly of interest to educators analyzing group results.

Percentile Rank

The percentile rank of your child's raw score on a test is simply *the percentage of students in the norm group whose test scores fall below your child's score.* (Percentile rank is not the same as a percentage score, which indicates what percent of the items were answered correctly.) For example, a child might answer eighty percent of the questions in a test correctly, but this raw score might place him at the seventieth percentile rank of the norm group. If your child's raw score had a percentile rank of seventy, then seventy of every one-hundred children in the norm group achieved a score below that of your child. Conversely, thirty percent of the norm group scored higher than your child.

One caution about interpreting changes in percentile ranks from year to year: Because test scores are typically clustered around the mean or average score, a very small change in raw score can produce a sizeable change in percentile scores near the fiftieth percentile. But it may take a larger change in raw score to produce much of a change in percentile score at either the upper or lower end of the score distribution. Thus if your third grade child achieves a percentile rank of fifty, compared to last year's percentile rank of forty on the same test, he has not demonstrated as much actual change as if his scores had gone from the eighty-fifth percentile to the ninety-fifth percentile. In fact, the fifty-to-forty score difference in the mid-range may not indicate any actual change, as will be explained below.

Grade Equivalents

Grade equivalent scores identify the school grade level at which the median test score is the same as that achieved by your child. A median score is the score in a distribution which has one-half of the remaining scores above it and the other half below it. Your child might achieve a grade equivalent score in reading comprehension of 3.0. This score would be correctly interpreted to mean that your child's reading comprehension is equivalent to that of the median beginning third-grader. However, you need to understand that a child who scores several grades above or below his present grade placement may not have the same knowledge or skills as all other students with the same score. A third-grader, for instance, with an arithmetic score of 6.0 and an eighth-grader with the same grade equivalent score do not necessarily have the same knowledge of mathematics. Likewise, it follows that this third-grader should not necessarily (nor typically) be handed a sixth-grade mathematics book.

Age Equivalents

Age equivalent scores allow you to identify the age of students to which your child's performance is most comparable. Thus your nine-year-old's math skills may be the equivalent of the average eleven-year-old, or her vocabulary may be similar to that of the average seven-year-old. The same limitations apply to age equivalents as to grade equivalents.

General Recommendations For Test Interpretation

In Chapter 6, I made some general recommendations to you about securing your child's standardized achievement test results and developing an understanding of their meaning. I can now expand upon those recommendations in light of the information presented thus far in this appendix.

1. Always establish what norm group(s) your child's performance is being compared to: local, state or national. You may be able to compare your child's performance to that of other children in your school, for example, as well as to children at the same grade level in your state and in the nation.

2. Ask about the standard error of measurement for the particular test (or subtest) your child took.

The standard error of measurement determines the width of the band of confidence in which your child's "true score" lies. We can be confident two out of three times, for example, that your child's true score lies within plus or minus one standard error of measurement. Thus if your child's score on a reading achievement test is seventy, and the standard error of measurement is five, we can be fairly confident (two out of three times) that her true score is somewhere between sixty-five and seventy-five. We can be more confident (ninety-five times out of one hundred) that her true score is somewhere between sixty and eighty.

3. Make certain that both you and your child's teacher consider the standard error of measurement as you interpret and discuss test results. Realize, for example, that a small increase from one year to the next in a child's reading comprehension score may or may not indicate any actual change, for the true scores may be identical. So if a teacher were using achievement test scores to place students in reading groups and if he bases placement upon single scores rather than bands of confidence, he may be placing some students in a group whose true skill levels in reading are higher than some of the students in the next higher level reading group. Ask your child's teacher what uses he makes of achievement test scores so you can make certain that your child is not being misplaced based upon improper test interpretation. Some teachers don't use the test scores for any purpose. When it comes to one-time, one-year test results, no use may be the best use, but you can consider ways that the results might support a point you want to make regarding your child's educational program, such as his reading group placement.

5. Maintain your own records of your child's yearly achievement test results and use them to spot trends—the year-by-year pattern of strengths and

weakness—which you may want to bring to the teacher's attention.

Remember that achievement test results are often, unfortunately, not fully understood by teachers, and may in fact be misinterpreted by them. As an interactive parent you should study and interpret the results yourself and then guard against their possible misinterpretation or misuse.

Appendix C

The Interactive Parent's Annual Calendar

As an interactive parent you will be involved with your child's education every month of the year. The calendar below gives you an annual perspective and serves as an ongoing checklist.

The calendar is based on a typical school year consisting of thirty-six weeks beginning on September 1st and ending on May 30th, but you can easily adapt it to your own child's school year. While the calendar starts in August, I encourage you to begin being an interactive parent as soon as you have read this book, regardless of the current date.

You won't want to wait to do something until it appears on the calendar if your situation requires you to act sooner. Assess the elements of your situation and decide when your actions will have the most beneficial effects. I especially urge you not to wait for the next parent-teacher conference if you believe that a real problem exists now, not to miss an opportunity to show your appreciation to school personnel, not to wait until "next year" to remove your child from the classroom of a teacher you now realize is incompetent. Do pay special attention, however, to suggestions in the calendar that you not do something during a given time period, such as scheduling a conference with a principal on the day before school begins.

Ask the school secretary for a copy of your school's annual calendar. Calendars for the upcoming school year are usually available in the spring. If you insert your calendar in a notebook, you can also insert pages for a log in which to record dates and notes of your interactions throughout the year.

Calendar of Actions and Interactions

August
(approximately two weeks before school starts)

1. Make positive contact with the school secretary, especially if she is new to the position or to you. Check to make certain that the teacher you helped select for your child is returning and is still assigned to the same grade. If the annual standardized achievement test results were not available at the end of the previous school year, secure a copy of your child's record now. Develop face and voice recognition with the secretary. Ask for the birthdates (month and day) of your child's teacher(s). Make an appointment for a brief visit with the principal.

2. Visit the principal, who will be on duty but probably not yet rushed. Establish (or reestablish) face and voice familiarity and help the principal renew his awareness of your child. Also reiterate the general message of an interactive parent. If a reassignment of your child to a new teacher has occurred or is imminent, you will need to deal with this problem immediately. Try not to have this visit with the principal later than one week before school begins and try to keep it positive.

3. If you have had no previous contact with her, make contact with your child's teacher four to eight days before the first day of school. Most teachers will be preparing their rooms even though they may have not yet formally begun work. The school secretary will know if your child's teacher has been at the school and can probably set up a convenient time for a visit. Avoid contact at school two or three days immediately prior to the first day of classes because teachers are usually tied up with inservice workshops and staff meetings on those days.

   Convey to the teacher the general message of an interactive parent and tell her you'll be looking for ways the two of you can best work together as partners in your child's education. Find out how you can most conveniently contact the teacher (time and method) when you need to, and let the teacher know that you welcome all communications (written notes, evening phone calls, etc.). Inquire about volunteering in the classroom or other ways of participating and about anything special the class may need for the instructional program which you might provide. Let her know you'd like to read the formal curriculum for your child's grade level, if you are not familiar with it, and ask about a convenient time for you to do so—suggest some time after the first couple weeks of school. During the first week of school, avoid more than momentary contact with the teacher, unless she requests a meeting, because she will be very busy and probably a little stressed as she tries to get to know her students and routinize classroom procedures.

4. If your child will be attending a new school or is apprehensive about school for any reason, visit the school with your child a few days before opening day to help him become acquainted with the layout of the building, the playground if he's an elementary student, the library, his classroom's location, and so on. You might ask the secretary for an okay, and then do keep your child in tow and avoid interrupting staff at work.

September

1. Become familiar with the curriculum for your child's grade. Make a copy of it for yourself if you can. Talk to your child daily about school and attempt to correlate what he's studying in each subject with the curriculum guide. Engage him in lots of lively, casual discussion related to those segments of the curriculum he is currently learning, find ways to relate the curriculum to life at home and in the community, and look for other ways to supplement and enrich his learning experiences. (Continue such at-home curricular support throughout the school year and into the

summer.) You can also use the curriculum guide to forecast (or ask the teacher to forecast) upcoming segments of the curriculum that will be covered in school so you can find ways to help your child build up a good background knowledge that will in turn help him learn the new curricular material.

2. Consider curriculum related items which you may be able to provide for your child's classroom. These need not be expensive, or even purchased. For example, an abandoned wasps' nest in your backyard may make a wonderful science exhibit; you may have an exciting math computer game that is in the public domain; a new piece of leftover carpet might make a fine rug for a reading corner. Continue to be aware of other ways you might contribute or participate.

3. Send a note to your child's teacher recognizing something he has done that especially pleased your child or you, like an exciting science demonstration or a field trip. Don't forget your child's other teachers here as well, such as the librarian or music or art teacher, and the principal, though it is usually wise to give primary attention to the regular classroom teacher. Continue this practice throughout the year.

October

1. Participate in a parent-teacher conference before your child's teacher gets involved in the end-of-the-quarter rush with report cards and regular parent-teacher conferences. (Don't wait till the quarter's end to find out how your child is doing in school.) Review your child's general adjustment to the new class, her academic progress, and raise any questions you have about the curriculum, teaching methods, classroom environment, and class schedule (which may involve other teachers). Pay particular attention to what your child will be studying the next few weeks in each subject area so that you can supplement at home. Mention those curriculum support ideas you previously generated and are using at home, and

offer a small menu of any curriculum related items you could supply.

If time permits, and if the teacher is prepared to do so, discuss your child's standardized achievement test results of the previous spring. (You may wish to have this be a topic for discussion at your next conference; just prior to regular parent-teacher conference time, teachers often prepare for reviewing test results.)

2. Take note of whether or not your child is using the school library. Determine if you need to encourage more use or ask his teacher about more frequent opportunities to check out books. Support his reading through reading and book discussions at home. Show an interest.

3. Consider the learning outcomes you have identified as being critical in your child's education. Consider the degree to which these are being addressed in your child's curriculum. If gaps exist, explore with school personnel possible ways in which the missing outcomes might be addressed at school. If none exist, consider how you can supplement the school's curriculum on your own.

4. If you spot problems, begin a problem-solving process, as outlined in Chapter 7.

November

1. Participate in your second parent-teacher conference approximately two weeks later than the regular parent-teacher conference week. Review your child's report card and secure information on upcoming areas of study. Discuss your child's mastery of those segments of the curriculum so far studied. Pay particular attention to the teacher's perceptions of your child's learning ability and to her levels of expectation for your child's achievement. If you have begun a problem-solving process for any reason, you may want to discuss it during this conference or schedule a separate problem-related conference.

2. Do something special for your child's teacher(s) this month. Perhaps you could be a special presenter, or arrange for a presentation by some expert in the community (a beekeeper, taxidermist, electrician, quilter, storyteller, author...). Personal items can be nice, too, based upon your growing knowledge of the teacher. Who wouldn't appreciate a beautiful fall bouquet on a crisp November morning? And remember the teacher's birthday.

2. If you have not done so previously, this is also a good time to hold a conference with any special teachers your child sees. Look at the grades your child received in classes taught by these teachers. Look for strengths and strong interests. Discuss your child with these teachers. Relate what is being taught in these special classes to the list of outcomes you have established for your child's education.

December

1. Give a Christmas gift to the teacher and possibly other school staff, if Christmas qualifies as a "special occasion" for them.

2. Arrange a pre-vacation conference, if you feel it would be beneficial, to check again on your child's progress on segments of the curriculum that will be begun after vacation (that you can be casually building background and interest for during vacation), and for any weak areas in your child's progress for which you might provide informal catch-up activities during vacation.

3. Follow-up on any problem-solving activities in progress.

January—February

1. Participate in a fourth parent-teacher conference a few weeks after Christmas break. Review your child's second quarter report card, preview upcoming areas of study, and pursue any other matters that concern you. By this time, having been interactive all fall, you

will probably be skilled at coming up with conference agenda items and at engaging in meaningful discussions with the teacher during conferences. The teacher, likewise, having now become familiar with you and your message, will be better able to meet your needs during conferences.

2. Make preliminary inquiry about which teachers will probably be teaching the subsequent grade the next year. Begin exploring the policies and procedures for assigning students to teachers. (Note: If the principal is new, do not assume that existing policies will be maintained, even if they are part of the school district's formal policy manual.)

3. Make some positive contact with the principal at this time. You will be dealing with him during upcoming weeks on the matter of teacher selection and will benefit if your relationship with him is familiar, friendly and cooperative.

4. If you've engaged in any problem-solving processes, be watchful in order to ensure the continuing effectiveness of solutions to problems. Take action if problems reoccur.

March

1. Continue to preview upcoming areas of study with your child's teacher. Continue supporting the curriculum at home with your child. Arrange conferences as needed. Send notes, volunteer, and otherwise participate as appropriate.

2. Begin your teacher selection process for the coming school year by confirming policies and procedures, gathering other people's opinions (be sure to include your child's present teacher), and making classroom observations. (See Chapter 3.)

April

1. Complete your teacher selection process by identifying the desired teacher, discussing your choice with

the teacher and principal, and getting confirmation of the placement.

2. Continue previewing topics of study for the remainder of the school year. Continue providing background experiences at home and monitoring curriculum mastery.

3. Maintain vigilant attention to your child's progress during this month and the next, a time when teachers and students sometimes wind down the pace. Remember (and help your child's teacher remember) that every teaching-learning moment is a valuable one.

May

1. Participate in a parent-teacher conference at least two weeks before school is out. Thank your child's teacher for a successful year, review new standardized achievement test results if they are available, and gather ideas for informal summer learning experiences for your child. Ask about book titles for recreational summer reading. Ask about any summer learning programs that might benefit your child.

2. Preview the curriculum for the next grade level to get additional ideas for fun, summertime academic background experiences. If next year's teacher is available, arrange a brief introductory meeting and talk with her about the upcoming curriculum.

June—July—August

1. Provide your child with all possible learning experiences that reinforce the previous year's curriculum or relate to next year's curriculum. For example, if your child will be studying U.S. history next year and you will be passing historical sites during a summer trip, stop to visit them. If learning to make change will be part of the math curriculum, encourage your child to "play store," and help him begin using money in real situations. Engage in loads of discussion to casually help him continue developing his oral language skills

(which will automatically, in turn, improve his writing skills) and casually use words that will expand his vocabulary.

2. Heed school news in the local paper, among friends, on local TV, among school board members, and so on. Has the teacher you selected for next year left the district or been given a different teaching assignment? Is a new principal coming to town? Such occurrences can require additional interaction on your part and are not something you want to learn about the day before school starts.

3. If a new principal or teacher is moving into your community, serve as part of the welcoming group or make a special individual effort to be a good neighbor or say hello. You may be dealing with these people at some time in the future.

4. Enjoy being your child's main teacher during the summer months; read, read, read together and talk, talk, talk together. Arrange special learning environments and experiences, with an emphasis on fun and informality, involving other kids as appropriate, make trips to the library, and once in a while discuss last year's schoolwork and review his portfolio of schoolwork if he has one.

As you read and reread *Getting the Best Bite of the Apple,* and as you practice interactive parenting, you'll find yourself adding to the above suggestions, moving dates around to fit your unique circumstances, and creating new ideas for helping your child learn.

Appendix D

Setting Standards for Exceptional Students

In Chapter 5 you learned about setting standards for your children's learning achievement within the context of new information about intellectual ability and expectation. Two groups of students may pose unique challenges in this respect, the intellectually gifted and the learning handicapped. This appendix will provide you guidance for dealing with such exceptions.

The Intellectually Gifted

Typically, *intellectually gifted* children are defined as those whose academic achievement or measured intelligence places them in the top three percent of their peer group. Because these students master skills so rapidly, they often create problems in the regular assembly line of institutional learning. Sometimes, too, they become bored with its pace, which is geared to the majority, to the perceived average, and in turn they can develop serious behavior problems or tune out. Studies indicate that as many as ten percent of the students who drop out of high school are intellectually gifted. At the elementary level, many gifted students are forced by circumstance to stifle or ignore some of their own curiosity and intellectual energy, and can lose their love of learning in the process.

We must first of all recognize that giftedness sometimes goes unrecognized. Your child may be the only person who knows he's gifted. You may suspect that he is, or, on the other hand, like many parents, let wishful thinking influence your perceptions so that you think he is, when he isn't. If your child does excellent daily work at school, consistently and proudly earns good grades, loves school, and is the teacher's delight, chances are high that he is *not* intellectually gifted. Because schools are not usually focused on the gifted nor flexible enough to accommodate the gifted, there is likely to be some sign of dissatisfaction, disruption, or imbalance. He is probably not being sufficiently challenged and stimulated and not allowed to use his full range of thinking skills.

To spot giftedness in your child, watch realistically for combinations of the following characteristics:

- teaches herself new skills, often with little or no assistance;

- prefers to work alone, and does not like to be interrupted when concentrating on a project;

- asks many questions about a large number of topics;

- expresses ideas well for her age level;

- demonstrates an excellent memory and an advanced vocabulary for her age level;

- grasps new ideas quickly;

- has a longer attention or concentration span than most children of her age;

- does not like routines and complains of boredom with repetitive activities.

If you suspect that your child is intellectually gifted, discuss this topic with one or more teachers. Don't necessarily expect them to be familiar with the above characteristics, but ask them questions related to the characteristics. *Does my child work alone a lot in class? Is it hard to pull her away from something she's concentrating on? How do her verbal skills compare with those of her classmates?* If you receive some confirmation of your own observations, you may wish to refer your child to the school's special education department for evaluation. Make your referral either through her teacher or her principal. You can also arrange for testing to be done privately. A word of caution, however. If your child is still in primary school and has enjoyed a rich learning environment in her preschool years, she will likely score well above average on an IQ test. She has been exposed to more learning-related experiences than have many of her peers. She has benefited from high expectations, frequent parental modeling, and a high value placed on learning. A high IQ score for such a child may well reflect these advantages and could easily decline by ten or more points upon retesting for continued program eligibility two or three years later.

If it turns out that your child has a number of the above characteristics and also a measured IQ in the 130+ range, the special education staff may make recommendations regarding changes in her education program. If they don't, or if you have the evaluation done privately, ask school staff what opportunities for intellectually gifted students exist at the school. You may be told that the school has no gifted program, or that the regular classroom teacher handles gifted students. (Translation: We have no program.) Or you may be informed that your child's school does have a special program, but that it starts in the fourth grade or at the high school level. Such a statement admittedly defies logic, since one does not become gifted only at a particular age or grade level. This position, however, may have been taken as a result of limited resources or to reflect experience with the "fading gifted" cited above. Of course, the school may in fact have a special program for your child.

If you had the evaluation done privately, take your documentation (IQ test results, etc.) with you for a conference with your child's regular classroom teacher. Show her your documents and ask for her response and advice. Ask the teacher if there are ways she might adjust classroom activities for your child. If you feel your child isn't being challenged enough, say so. In recent years, education researchers have nudged teachers towards greater flexibility with respect to individual student needs, and you may be lucky enough to have an enlightened teacher on hand. If you aren't, you'll need to take further steps, up the ante, so to speak, applying interactive pressure on the teacher and probably the principal. You will want to generate some ideas yourself before approaching school staff again, consult your child about her wants and needs, check your state laws regarding gifted programs (which are in many states mandated), and then use the problem-solving process outlined in this book as you forge ahead.

If a separate, special program for the gifted does exist at your school, begin gathering information about how it is run, what it includes, and how adaptable and stimulating it is. Talk with parents of children who are in the program, and with their children as well. Also interview the teacher assigned to the program. Ask him how the program is implemented, whether or not your child's involvement would cause her to miss part of the regular curriculum, and whether or not the program will help bring about adjustments in her regular classroom activities. You'll need to use the information you gather to determine whether or not the program has the qualities you think your child needs. Unfortunately, some gifted programs are shallow, inflexible, don't individualize, or are taught by un-gifted teachers! Many gifted programs involve students in a one-hour-a-week activity but do nothing to modify a child's program the other twenty-nine hours, and some schools offer the same canned program to all participants within particular grade levels. The best programs tap each gifted student's personal educational interests and custom-design educational plans for each. The plans vary widely and sometimes venture into areas completely omitted from the regular curriculum, areas as diverse as radio technology, advanced cello, rocketry, or oceanography.

If you are advised that your child's school does not have a gifted program, you have a choice to make. You may elect to drop the matter as far as the school is concerned, locate separate resources, familiarize yourself with gifted-education processes, and establish your own program for your child outside of the regular school day, handled by you or others (in, for example, a mentor-apprentice situation). Or you may establish a full-time home school or locate a private school for gifted students.

On the other hand, you may elect to press the school for appropriate services. Refer to your state's gifted-education laws and find out how your state regulates and oversees gifted education. Find out if your school district has its own gifted-education policies. Read them, inquire about how they are carried out, use them to further your cause. Realize that doing all of this may place you in a confrontation mode with school personnel. In that case, look to Chapter 7 for a review of both the process and likely outcomes of confrontation, so you can make a wise decision about whether and how to proceed.

The key here is your child. What will be best for her? Leaving a gifted child to flounder in a regular program can be dangerous—she may, as noted above, at the least grow bored, at the worst become rebellious. Almost always, she will be sad.

You need to be aware that some public educators do not like gifted children. Those children who do not fit into the common mold create extra demands on what may be an already overwhelmed teacher. The teacher may simply not be as intellectually bright as the child and may not understand the gifted child's need to question or to perceive problems and information in unusual ways, to be active and curious, and to do things his own way.

The system, too, can disfavor the gifted. As we know, mediocrity can abhor excellence, and often the majority favors the underdog. Schools are by nature egalitarian— education for all; everyone is equal. Applying special funds and efforts to gifted programs can actually anger some people, including some school officials who are frequently looking for ways to cut the budget. Those cuts often come where the fewest are involved, and the gifted are the fewest.

But again, remember the key issue: your child. While successful interactive parents avoid soapboxes, they do remain committed, taking those informed, planned, multiple, and consistent steps described throughout this book to see that their children get the best available educations.

The Learning Handicapped

Typically, five to ten percent of any school's students are considered by educators to be *learning handicapped*. This label covers categories of students who do not progress satisfactorily, or for whom special services are necessary to allow progress. Historically, these categories consisted of the mentally retarded, physically handicapped, and emotionally disturbed. Then in 1973, federal law mandated special services for all learning-handicapped children and provided federal funds for implementation. Rapidly, the ranks of special education students in the public school system swelled, due in large part, of course, to the law, but also to a new education malady simultaneously gaining recognition called *learning disabilities*. This label was soon applied to thousands of youngsters who were doing poorly in the nation's public schools, but who could not be fitted into one of the more historically accepted categories. While the number of handicapped students as a percent of the total student population remained stable in the historical categories, the number in this new category, the learning disabled, rose between 1976 and 1982 from 1.8 percent of all students to 4.4 percent—an increase of almost a million children.

Why the great "success" of the learning disabilities movement? It provided a means of placing more children in special education programs, funded by more federal and state dollars, and generated a need for more special education teachers. Besides that, it made parents and teachers more comfortable. A regular classroom teacher now could say he knew why a given child wasn't achieving and could himself assume less responsibility. It also supplied a reason to send the child out of the classroom (to the special education resource room) with a clear conscience (and an easier load). The parent was relieved to learn that the child's malady had been diagnosed and was being treated. A new group of educators emerged, wrapped in the professional magic of the medical model. Everyone gained—except children. Over time since the '70s, research has demonstrated that the majority of students placed in special education classrooms—with specially trained teachers, special instructional materials, and small pupil-teacher ratios—learn less and feel less positive and optimistic about themselves than do students *with the same learning difficulties* but left in the regular classroom.

If you have a handicapped child, especially one labeled "learning disabled," your interests as an interactive parent will probably be in basic conflict with those of the regular classroom teacher. You are interested in maximizing the learning of your child; the teacher is interested in maximizing the learning of the entire class. To do so, she probably directs her instruction at the average and wants to keep doing so. Her constant frustration over trying to move along the lame and the strays silently urges her to remove one or two youngsters from the classroom, if she can, and allow the rest of the group to maintain its pace. Admittedly, this is not an admirable practice, but given the overpopulated, lightly staffed classrooms that exist in many of our schools today, it is understandable. You, however, while able to understand it, must, for the sake of your child, consider circumventing it.

In other words, if you have a child designated "learning disabled," you should be skeptical about the special program that will be prescribed, particularly if it is to be carried out in the resource room. But you don't want your child to experience routine put-downs in the regular classroom either (though being forced to leave the regular classroom may be the biggest put-down he will experience). You're going to have to look honestly at your child, at the regular and resource room programs that are available to him, and consider your options.

After twenty years, educators are still arguing over a workable definition of this category. In addition, the field of learning disabilities has been plagued with a series of ineffectual educational remedies. Although their continuation is often guaranteed by the gap of ten to fifteen years it takes educational research recommendations to result in improved teaching practices, research has shown many prescribed intervention strategies to be worthless.

If your child is what I refer to as a true special education child—is physically handicapped, mentally retarded, or emotionally disturbed—you will probably be pleased with the services many schools provide. These students comprise only about twenty-five percent of special education students. Pushed by Public Law 94-142, school districts have taken positive steps to provide many needed services, such as physical therapy or large print books. Often they also integrate or "mainstream" these special education youngsters into the regular classroom—a research-supported practice. Truly handicapped students can indeed be the underdogs, and many teachers do all within their power to help. Nevertheless, even in these cases, parents need to maintain close contact with the school to see that required services are beneficial and delivered.

The above comments are intended to alert you to some of the circumstances, good or bad, that you may face if your youngster is fitted into one of the special education categories. You'll want to examine in detail and with honesty the current values of variables (ability, expectation, and achievement) in your child's education program, reevaluate any standards you have set or set some, gather information, and either enter the problem-solving mode outlined in this book or confirm for yourself that your child is indeed receiving the best available education.

GLOSSARY

ability groups (see *instructional groups)*

ability level The maximum level at which a child is believed able to perform successfully due to intelligence (IQ) and previous learning. (see also *expectation)*

accountability Teachers' ability to prove that their students have mastered all or most of the material outlined in a curriculum. A term used by parents and legislators to express a desire to have greater knowledge of what schools are accomplishing.

achievement test (see *standardized achievement test; criterion-referenced test)*

ACT American College Testing. The widely used ACT college-entrance exam tests a student's general knowledge and skills in English, math, social studies and natural science.

administrator A school's supervisory level personnel, such as a superintendent, principal, or vice principal.

AFT American Federation of Teachers, the second largest teachers' union in the U.S.

alternative education Schooling options within public schools (school-within-a-school concept) or outside of the public system, such as private, parochial, and home schools.

alternative school A school established within a public school district that provides an education program atypical of other schools in the district. Alternative schools may espouse a particular educational philosophy or methodology, e.g., basic education, Montessori; or be designed for a particular type of student, e.g., at risk high school students or students talented in science or the arts.

apprenticeship A learning program in which a learner observes, is taught by, and works alongside of a mentor, that is, an adult who is skilled in the field under study.

assessment Ongoing observation of a student's work, test results, and/or application of skills and knowledge to holistic tasks in order to determine learning progress or achievement.

authentic assessment (see *performance-based assessment*)

basic education (basic skills) Core courses or subjects taught in a school, such as reading, math, social studies, and science; and basic or common skills within those core subjects, such as addition, subtraction, division, and multiplication in math.

behavioral objective (see *learning objective)*

CAT California Achievement Test, a commonly used standardized achievement test.

certification The formal licensing of a person to teach or perform other professional duties assigned to school personnel. Certification is usually granted in specific grade, position or subject areas, such as elementary, high school science, counselor, K-12 music, and principal and must be renewed by the holder after a time period which varies from state to state.

Chapter I A federally funded education program which provides supplementary assistance to "disadvantaged students" (low socioeconomic level students).

classroom curriculum That portion of a district's official curriculum which a teacher actually delivers to students. The classroom curriculum may fall short of the complete official curriculum or be embellished by incidental and "hidden" curricula.

classroom management The manner in which a teacher arranges students, instructional materials, time, student movement, other staff, etc., for procedural efficiency and to maximize learning time.

code of ethics (for teachers) Each state's adopted standards of ethical behavior for teachers (e.g., Teachers will not discuss a student's personal or school life with anyone other than parents, appropriate school personnel, and/or the child himself.)

competency testing The testing of potential and/or presently certified teachers to determine whether or not they possess basic English language and mathematical skills, often at approximately an 8th to 10th grade level.

competency-based education Education in which the outcome is measured by the learner's ability to demonstrate specific skills or knowledge, as opposed to education in which effects are measured by the amount of time spent exposed to instruction. (e.g., the requirement that eighth graders be able to write a composition which meets acceptable standards—under exam conditions—before entrance into ninth grade vs. entrance based upon the completion of eight years of schooling)

computer-assisted instruction (CAI) Learning in which computer activities are used (along with other activities) to help students learn subject matter skills, concepts, and processes.

computer education Classes or activities that focus on how to use computers, peripheral hardware (such as a printer) and computer software, and perhaps to learn computer programming. *Computer literacy*; that is, knowing basic terminology and functions, is the minimum goal of computer education.

cooperative learning Learning activities carried out cooperatively (not competitively) by students, and, in fact, whose success depends upon cooperative effort.

coordinator An administrative-level staff member whose function is ancillary or supportive rather than supervisory (e.g., special programs coordinator).

core curriculum Subjects considered *central* in a district's curriculum, such as reading and math, social studies and science. (see also *integrated curriculum*)

corporal punishment Physical punishment, such as spanking.

criterion-referenced test (CRT) An achievement test described in terms of the number of correct responses each student makes. CRTs enable an instructor to determine whether a student has adequately mastered a given set of skills. The student's performance is measured against a standard rather than compared to the achievement of other students.

CST Child study team, a group consisting of a child's teacher(s), principal, parent(s) and one or more special education personnel (teacher, school psychologist, etc.) who jointly make decisions about the instructional program of an exceptional child. (see also *IEP*; *Public Law 94-142*)

CTBS Comprehensive Test of Basic Skills, a commonly used standardized achievement test.

curriculum guide A book or notebook, typically prepared by a school district, containing educational objectives or outcomes that the district wants students to achieve. Teachers are generally expected to teach to these objectives or outcomes.

curriculum mastery A high degree of competence demonstrated by a student with the skills and knowledge (objectives and outcomes) of a district's curriculum and of an understanding of the concepts included in that curriculum.

diagnosis and prescription An ongoing process of testing (diagnosing) students' skills and designing instruction (prescribing) to meet an individual's learning needs.

direct instruction Instruction involving teacher-student interaction.

director A district's supervisor of a special program, such as special education. A director often has authority over ancillary program specialists, such as a school psychologist, but not over teachers or actual school operations.

early childhood education Educational programs geared to preschool through third graders, often based upon the research-supported principles espoused by the National Association for the Education of Young Children as "Appropriate Practices."

educationally-deprived child A child who has not had the "normal" preschool or out-of-school learning experiences and hence is not as prepared for public school as other children. Socioeconomic class and culture are often factors.

emotionally-disturbed child A child whose state of emotional health requires special instruction or other services to enable him to achieve an acceptable level of academic progress.

engaged time That time during which a student is actively learning or trying to learn, when he is *participating* in a learning activity. Research shows that *engagement* is the key to learning. (see also *learning time*; *instructional time*)

ESL English as a second language. Instruction in the English language for students whose first or primary language is not English.

evaluation of students Testing or other observational data-gathering that provides school personnel (and parents) with indicators of a child's ability or achievement level and of the efficacy of an education program.

evaluation of teachers A process through which a principal attempts to determine the degree of an individual teacher's instructional competence and to bring about continuous improvement. The process is usually formally prescribed in school district policies and/or in a negotiated agreement (labor contract).

exceptional child A child who is either gifted or handicapped to the extent that modifications of the school's regular instructional program are necessary for the child to satisfactorily develop educationally.

expectation The level of achievement conveyed to a child by a teacher or parent as acceptable or praiseworthy. Research shows that high expectation usually elicits high achievement, low elicits low, and so on.

extracurricular School activities offered in addition to instruction in the regular curriculum. (e.g., sports)

extrinsic reward A reward that comes from outside an activity (like a sticker from the teacher or an A grade) vs. a reward that comes from doing the activity (like a *feeling* of success or the satisfying realization that you *know* something new). Research shows that extrinsic rewards may actually diminish quality of performance and subsequent interest. (see also *intrinsic reward*)

faculty A school's certified *teaching* staff.

functional illiteracy The inability to read or write well enough to function normally in the practical world.

gifted student A student whose learning ability and/or achievement in one or more academic areas is sufficiently high to require modification of his instructional program to accommodate his giftedness. Each state and/or school district utilizes its own criteria for defining giftedness, such as a minimum score on a specified IQ test and academic ranking in the top three percent of students.

grade equivalent score (GE) A standardized test score that indicates the grade and month in school of students in the norm group whose median test performance matches that of the test taker. For example, if a third grade student's GE in a given subject is 5.4, her score matches the median score of students in the fourth month of the fifth grade. (This is *not* an indication that she should be placed in the fifth grade.)

graded classrooms Classes established by progress through grade one, grade two, grade three, and so on, with the greatest common denominator being students' chronological ages. (see also *nongraded classrooms)*

grouping (See *instructional groups.)*

handicapped child A child who needs a special education program in order to reach his educational potential as determined by a child-study team (CST) who consider his academic strengths and weakness and special needs. Further, a child who meets one of several definitions of the handicapped, in categories such as mentally retarded, emotionally disturbed, learning disabled.

hidden curriculum Information and attitudes informally disseminated among students by their peers or by school personnel that is not part of a school's stated (official) or unstated curriculums.

home school Schooling whereby parents teach their own children at home.

IEP Individual education program. A formal, annual statement of a special education student's instructional goals and objectives and the activities planned to achieve these objectives. The IEP is formulated by a child study team, requires parental approval (with rare exception), and contains means for evaluating the plan's success. (see also *CST; Public Law 94-142)*

illiterate, illiteracy Inability to read or write. (see also *functional illiteracy)*

independent work Work completed alone, or mostly alone, by a student. (e.g., an assignment completed by a student at her own desk with little or no assistance)

individualized instruction Instruction specially designed to meet observed individual student needs. (Sometimes mistakenly understood to be instruction provided one-on-one for an individual student.)

instructional groups Groups of students who work together on a learning task, usually students whose levels of achievement in a given subject are similar.

instructional level The level at which a student is able to understand new material being presented by a teacher or with a teacher's help, usually a level above a student's independent work level.

instructional time In-class time during which students actually receive instruction. (see also *engaged time*; *learning time*)

integrated curriculum Teaching more than one subject at a time or involving students in activities that require the application of skills and knowledge from more than one subject (e.g., a project that requires discussion skills, graphics or artwork, and writing during the planning stages, plus math and science knowledge during both the planning and implementing stages, plus public speaking during the presentation stage.) Research indicates that student learning increases when subject matter is taught in an integrated manner because students can interrelate inter-curricular concepts and can recognize crossover uses of skills.

intelligence A student's capacity for understanding, learning, reasoning or thinking critically. A student's score on an IQ test has been traditionally thought of as a quantified and fixed intelligence level—see Chapter 5.

intermediate Traditionally grades four, five, and six. Sometimes grade six is included in middle school and grade three is included in intermediate.

intervention strategies Modifications in teaching techniques or other actions by school personnel used to intervene when either a student's rate of learning or in-school behavior becomes unacceptable.

intrinsic reward A reward that naturally comes out of engaging in an activity (like a child's *pleasure* at successfully solving a riddle or *feeling proud* about the sand castle he just built) vs. a reward given by someone else.

However, a second person may verbally confirm an intrinsic reward—"How proud you must feel, Joe!" —which is then intrinsically acknowledged—"Yes, I do!" (see also *extrinsic reward*)

ITBS Iowa Test of Basic Skills, a commonly used standardized achievement test.

junior high Grades seven and eight, and sometimes nine.

learning disability A malady ascribed to children placed in special education who are not academically successful in school; do not meet the definitions of other special education categories; whose learning problems are ostensibly not attributable to differences in language, culture or other environmental factors; and for whom a significant discrepancy between ability and achievement is identified.

learning objectives Specific skills which a student needs to master as steps towards a broader learning goal. (see also *learning outcomes)*

learning outcomes What students will *know and be able to do* once they have completed a series of learning activities. *Exit outcomes* describe the end product of a given level of schooling such as elementary or high school; *program outcomes* describe the knowledge and abilities a student is to master in a given program such as science or language arts. (see also learning objectives)

learning time Time when students are expected to be attempting to master learning objectives or reaching outcomes. True learning time requires learner *engagement* in the activity. (see also *instructional time*; *engaged time*)

least-restrictive environment Refers to the placement of a learning-handicapped child in a learning situation as much like that experienced by nonhandicapped children as possible while still enabling the learner to accomplish his learning objectives. (see also *mainstreaming*; *IEP)*

lesson plan A teacher's written design for a lesson; includes one or more learning objectives. (Typically teachers write, in advance, lesson plans in each subject for an entire week.)

literate, literacy Able to read and write.

mainstreaming The inclusion of learning-handicapped students in regular classroom learning activities to the greatest extent possible.

manipulative learning Instruction that includes much handling, exploring, and manipulating of real objects.

mental age The age of a child stated in terms of his mental capacity, as determined by comparing his assessed mental ability with the age at which the average child has the same ability. Thus a child with a chronological age of 8.5 might have, for example, a mental age of 7.0 or 9.3.

mentally retarded Children whose general intellectual functioning is in the lowest 2.5 percent of their age group as measured by an IQ test and who have been unable to learn expected academic and social skills, and for whom these deficits are not due to cultural or linguistic differences.

mentoring (see *apprenticeship*)

MAT Metropolitan Achievement Test, a commonly used standardized achievement test.

middle school Typically a school which includes grades six, seven and eight and espouses a particular educational philosophy and instructional program designed specifically for early adolescents.

motivation system Means by which school staff attempt to foster interest in and enthusiasm for learning, but which often are really attempts to control student behavior. Commonly used means are verbal praise, stickers (the new gold stars), grades, threats, loss of privileges, and suspension. (see also *extrinsic motivation*; *intrinsic motivation*)

National Education Association (NEA) A teacher organization which is the largest and one of the most powerful labor unions in the United States.

nongraded classrooms Classrooms not organized by grade level, but rather by such criteria as students' interests and achievement levels in given subjects. Students in nongraded classrooms may move from one room to another and back again throughout the school day.

normal curve equivalent (NCE) A standardized test score that ranges from 1 to 99 and coincides with national percentile scores at 1, 50, and 99, and which may be mathematically manipulated for comparison purposes. NCE's are predominantly used to determine student's baseline achievement and eventual progress in supplementary programs such as Chapter 1 and in reports submitted for federally funded programs.

official curriculum Written academic goals or outcomes, usually arranged by subject area, and either recommended or mandated by a district school board.

official policy Written policies officially adopted by a district's school board.

on-task time (see *engaged time*)

open classrooms Educationally, this term refers to classrooms whose staff and students are involved in interclass projects, exchanges and interactions. Architecturally, classrooms that are not entirely enclosed, but that are open to a central walkway or other common space, such as a library.

outcomes-based education (see *learning outcomes*)

parent rights Legally mandated rights of public school parents, such as the right to review a child's school records, have a child evaluated for special education services, or to visit any classroom.

parent-principal conference A formal meeting between a school's principal and a child's parent(s) for the purpose of resolving a problem that exists in the child's educational program which the parent is unable to resolve at a lower level of the educational hierarchy.

parent-teacher conference A meeting between one or both parents and a child's teacher, typically scheduled by school personnel at the end of the first quarter of the school year (and sometimes subsequent quarters) for the purpose of presenting an overview of a child's instructional program and indicating the child's progress. Sometimes additional problem-solving conferences are held.

parochial school A school operated by a religious organization.

percentile score A test score that reflects the percentage of students in a norm group who correctly answered fewer test questions than did the test-taker whose score is being referred to. The norm group may represent other children in your child's school, your state, or in the nation.

performance-based assessment Determining the extent of students' achievement by having them perform whole tasks that require the use of many specific skills and concepts (vs. assessing the skills and concepts one-by-one). Performance-based assessments attempt to see not just what students have learned but also how well they can apply what they've learned to realistic or authentic and holistic situations.

portfolio A collection of a student's work that can be used for ongoing assessment of progress and for the pleasure of reviewing as if it were a scrapbook.

prescriptive teaching (see *diagnosis and prescription*)

primary Grades kindergarten, one, two, and usually three.

principal A school's chief administrative officer, responsible for the overall operation of a school. This responsibility includes the supervision of all personnel, budget and physical plant management, instructional leadership, and community relations. Research shows that the instructional leadership skills of a principal are key to a school's academic achievement.

private school A school established and operated by a private group (rather than by the government) and which typically espouses a common educational philosophy and/or value system.

PTA Parent-Teacher Association. A group of teachers and parents who offer various kinds of support to schools and school programs.

Public Law 94-142 The Education for All Handicapped Children Act passed by Congress in 1975. This legislation was designed to ensure that handicapped students throughout the nation received appropriate educational services.

readiness The degree to which a child is prepared or has sufficient experiential background for kindergarten and first grade academics and socialization.

reinforcement Any response to a behavior which increases the strength or duration of the behavior or the probability of its reoccurrence. *Positive reinforcement* is a response which a child likes, such as candy for good behavior. *Negative reinforcement* is the removal of something which a child does *not* like, such as releasing a child from being "grounded" after three days of good behavior.

resource room A classroom where a special education teacher provides instruction to learning disabled, otherwise handicapped, and sometimes gifted children. A student's visits to the resource room may be for one or more subjects (typically reading and math) and often vary in length from twenty minutes to two or more hours per day.

restructuring The complete redesign of the existing educational system as opposed to reforming, or repairing, the system through minor change.

rote learning Learning by memorization only.

SAT Scholastic Aptitude Test; a verbal and mathematical aptitude test given to high school students and used as a predictor of college success.

school board Elected officials who are responsible for the overall operation of a school district. (May also be referred to as directors or trustees.) A school board's main responsibilities include policy making, goal setting, the hiring of a district superintendent, budget approval, and responding to public input.

school counselor A specially trained, certified school employee who counsels students regarding a range of issues such as vocational choice and social/emotional problems.

school nurse A professional nurse employed by a school to conduct health screenings, maintain student health records, treat minor illnesses and injuries, administer doctor-prescribed medications, and sometimes offer health-related education to students and/or teachers.

school psychologist A certified educational specialist trained in psychology. The individual who administers psychological evaluations and IQ tests, usually related to the consideration of a student for special education.

school secretary The secretary to a school principal and often the regulator of a school's daily routine. (An important ally for an interactive parent.)

secondary (high school) Grades nine, ten, eleven, and twelve. In some school districts grades seven and eight are also designated as *secondary*.

social behavior A student's interactions with his peers and with school personnel in the normal routine of a school day.

social promotion The passing of a student from one grade to another even though the student has not mastered the year's curriculum. Social promotion is usually justified by reference to a student's chronological age or physical size, a limited probability of academic success through retention, or the potential emotional damage resulting from retention.

special education Legally mandated education programs for students who are defined as learning handicapped, that is, mentally-retarded, emotionally disturbed, learning disabled, etc; and in some states for intellectually gifted students. (see also *Public Law 94-142)*

special programs Federally funded educational programs with a specific focus and purpose, such as Chapter I, Indian Education, and special education.

specialist An educator who has received concentrated training in a specific area. (e.g., a reading specialist)

speech therapist Specially trained person who treats children with speech defects.

standard A *performance* standard defines how well students are expected to perform assessment tasks in order to demonstrate mastery of intended outcomes. A *content* standard refers to what students should know and be able to do in a given academic discipline (content area) and is synonymous with what some educators refer to as program outcomes.

standardized achievement test A test which measures academic achievement, which is given under the same conditions at each testing site (hence is "standardized"), and which has "norms" which enable comparisons among students' test results. (See Appendix B.)

Stanford Achievement Test A commonly used standardized achievement test.

State Commissioner of Education The executive officer of a state's Department of Education; usually selected by and responsible to a state Board of Education.

State Department of Education The division of state government which administers public education in a given state. Responsibilities typically include the licensing (certification) of all professional educational personnel, managing the state's funding of school districts, promulgating regulations that guide the implementation of educational practices mandated by state statutes, and providing technical assistance to school districts.

student rights Legal and other rights guaranteed to all students by the Constitution and federal statutes, by state laws governing public education, and possibly by school district policies.

superintendent The executive officer of a school district, responsible for the administration of a school district's entire education program. The superintendent is hired by and responsible to the district school board.

teacher aide A person who assists a teacher in various ways, such as creating bulletin boards, correcting papers, supervising students, teaching small groups, and so on.

teacher association (see *National Education Association; American Federation of Teachers*)

textbook series A series of books in one subject area, one text for each ability or grade level, published by one publishing company. (Students progress from text to text as they move from level to level or grade to grade.)

tracking The practice of placing students in classrooms, specific classes, or educational programs based upon perceived learning ability or past academic performance.

transition time The time required for students to move from one learning activity to another; a part of non-learning time.

unofficial policy Customary practices established informally by school personnel and carried on as tradition.

unstated curriculum The set of values which school personnel both consciously and unconsciously attempt to inculcate in their students.

vice principal An administrative officer who is often assigned specific administrative responsibilities within a school, such as extracurricular activities or discipline.

volunteer aide A volunteer, typically a student's parent, who works in a school as an unpaid teacher's helper in varying capacities.

whole-group activity Lessons taught to an entire class at the same time.

whole language An educational philosophy, particularly applicable to elementary school classes, which is evident in classrooms where students are taught to read and write in large part through holistic tasks and situations. For example, instead of step-by-step intensive phonics instruction, you'll see students learning phonics in the context of whole pieces of writing, or books, whereby the students' attempts to use phonics skills are supported by the meaning of a line or passage.

WISC The Wechsler Intelligence Scale for Children, the intelligence test most commonly used in public schools.

INDEX

manipulative learning, 142
mastery learning
  see curriculum mastery
measurement
  see test
  see also test score
  see also standard error of
    measurement
mediocrity, 55, 61, 95
mental age, 142
mentally retarded
  see handicapped students
monitoring progress
  see achievement, monitor-
    ing
motivation, student, 25,
    33-35, 58, 59, 142, 145
  extrinsic, 138
  intrinsic, 140-141
  see also expectation,
    teacher

N
NEA (National Education
    Association)
  see union, teachers'
negotiation, 58, 74-75, 80-
    81, 82, 83, 84
nongraded classroom, 142
  see also graded classroom
norm group, 54, 66, 109,
    111-112
normal curve equivalent
  see test score
nurse, school, 12-13, 30, 146

O
objectives
  see learning objectives
    and outcomes

observation, of classroom
  see selection, of teacher
official curriculum
  see curriculum
official policy
  see policy
on-task time
  see engaged time
open classrooms, 143
opinions
  of "experts", 8, 27-28, 32,
    72, 79, 92, 95, 121
  of other parents, 29-31,
    86, 121
outcomes-based education
  see learning objectives
    and outcomes
overachiever, 59

P
Parenting magazine, 7
parent rights
  see law, and parent rights
parent-principal conference,
    17-19, 38-39, 80-81,
    115, 116
  see also principal
Parent-Teacher Association,
    9, 145
parent-teacher conference,
    8, 15-19, 22, 38-39, 63,65-
    66, 67, 80-81, 115, 118-119,
    120-121, 122, 127, 144
  see also communication
  see also specific topics
peer interaction, 36, 44-45,
    107
peers, comparison with, 54,
    58, 59, 61, 109, 111, 112,
    125, 126, 127